Teaching Your Child Creativity

A  Guide

Teaching Your Child Creativity

Lee Hausner, Ph.D.

Jeremy Schlosberg

LifeLine
Press
Washington, DC

Copyright © 1998 by Affinity Communications Corp.

Library of Congress Cataloging-in-Publication Data

Hausner, Lee.
  Teaching your child creativity : a Playskool guide / Lee Hausner, Jeremy Schlosberg.
          p.   cm.
    Includes index.
    ISBN 0-89526-434-X (pbk.)
    1. Creative activities and seat work. 2. Early childhood education—Activity programs. 3. Early childhood education—Parent participation. 4. Creative ability. I. Schlosberg, Jeremy, 1958- . II. Title.
    LB1140.35.C74H38 1997
    649'.51—dc21   97-37771

Published in the United States by
LifeLine Press
An Eagle Publishing Company
1 Massachusetts Avenue, NW
Washington, DC 20001

Distributed to the trade by
National Book Network
4720-A Boston Way
Lanham, MD 20706

Books are available in quantity for promotional or premium use. Write to LifeLine Press, 1 Massachusetts Avenue, NW, Washington, DC 20001, for information on discounts and terms or call (202) 216-0600.

9/98
B&T

Contents

Foreword

As the creators of Playskool® products, creativity is our link to the millions of children who play with our toys, and to the families and friends who observe, encourage, and participate in a child's play.

Without creativity, the world as we know it would not exist. Imagine a world without electricity, light bulbs, refrigeration, automobiles, antibiotics, bicycles, computers, telephones, radio, and television—all by-products of the creative ingenuity of ordinary people.

We, the makers of Playskool® products, are constantly striving to develop new and exciting products that are ever more challenging, dynamic, and fun. Of course, as we encourage children to be creative, we can only supply some of the tools. Much of the task has to be left to family, friends, and teachers. But the most important role can be played by the parent or primary caregiver. Creativity thrives on encouragement, and there is no better source of encouragement than from a parent or primary caregiver.

We encourage you to take the time to expose your children to the wonderful world of creativity. It may be the most rewarding gift you'll ever give them.

Margaret C. Whitman
General Manager, Playskool®

PART ONE

Creativity Can Be Taught (By You!)

CHAPTER ONE

The Power of Creativity

"Man is happiest when he is creating."
—LEO BUSCAGLIA

Give her some big crayons and a large sheet of paper, and your two-year-old will go to town: scribbles here, loops there, zigzags over everything. She might use a lot of colors, or she might stay with whatever she grabs first.

What she draws may look like random squiggles, but she'll adore it. And you, as a good parent, will coo and smile and acknowledge her joy. "What a wonderful drawing!" you might say. Or, "I love what you've done!"

Or you might simply exclaim: "How creative!" because parental instinct tells you that "creative" is good and should be encouraged.

That parental instinct is correct. It has been borne out through extensive research which suggests that the more creative you are, the greater your potential for high levels of achievement and fulfillment in life. Without creativity, even children with above average IQs may have a difficult time living up to their potential, especially *after* they finish school and start on the rest of their lives and careers.

On the job and in life, creativity is just as important as classroom skills. Numerous studies show that traditional indicators of academic success—such as doing well on tests or having an "A" average—rarely are the best predictors of future success.

That's because there is another powerful factor at work in almost every task of life: Creativity.

In recent years, we have come to learn that no matter what your child's interests or future career choices are, creativity is extremely important. For example, we know that creative children are more likely to become creative, productive, and successful adults.

We also know a great deal about how to identify and encourage creativity in children; we know the habits and tendencies of creative people; and we know how to encourage those habits and tendencies in children.

And guess what—that's great news, because creativity can be taught. It's not even hard. In fact, it's fun.

And this book can teach you how.

The result will enrich your child's life—and your own—immeasurably, both personally and professionally. In fact, you'll find that this book will help you talk with your children and help them tell you what's on their minds.

By now I hope you are asking what this thing called creativity is. Or you might even be thinking: "Wait a second, I *know* what creativity is. That's what artists have—novelists, poets, painters. And a lot of them die miserable and broke. What does that have to do with my child's future?"

Well, many artists are creative in a certain way. But creativity is not just for the arts or for artists. Not at all. What we mean by creativity in this context—the force or ability that is so important to later success in life—is very different from just being good at arts and crafts.

We'll give a full definition of creativity—and the reasoning behind it—in the next chapter. But for now, just to understand why creativity is so important to your child, think of creativity as being a bit like what some people used to call "Yankee ingenuity." (At least that's what some Yankees called it!)

Creative people have a powerful drive to make things better—whether the "thing" is a mousetrap, a symphony, a drag racer, or a microchip. They are good at making things better not only because they are open to new answers but also because they are good at changing around the questions. And once they see the answer, they don't stop at theory—

> Creativity can be taught. It's not even hard. In fact, it's fun.

they have the drive to put their ideas into action. After all, there is no creativity unless something is created.

Michelangelo was creative. So was Beethoven. But as at least one group of researchers in the subject has pointed out, one of the most creative men in history was Sikorsky, the inventor of the helicopter.

For decades after the Wright brothers, the size and weight of an airplane that could take off from a given location was limited by the length of the runway. True, many talented and inventive people addressed the problem and made improvements—better wing design, lighter materials, more powerful engines, even catapults, all to shorten the distance the plane had to travel along the ground until the air was rushing past the wings fast enough to lift the plane.

It was Sikorsky who thought "outside the box," who changed not only the answer but the question. For a helicopter the question is not how far the plane has to go to get the wind moving past the wings, but how fast the "wings" can spin around on top of the "plane"! All of a sudden the answer to

"How long does the runway need to be?" was "We don't need a runway at all!"

That's creativity.

When we think of creativity that way is it any wonder that corporate America is rediscovering the benefits of having a creative work force? In fact more and more companies are now teaching grown-ups (often through games and exercises

Is creativity important in adult life? If the company you keep is any indication, then considering that American Express, Apple computer, AT&T, CBS, Coca-Cola, General Electric, Hewlett-Packard, IBM, NASA, NBC, and Procter & Gamble have held creativity workshops for their employees, the answer is a resounding yes! Why? Richard Restak, M.D., associate professor of neurology at the Georgetown University School of Medicine, says that one of the main reasons that people wish to be creative is because they understand that creativity can help them attain almost any goal they set for themselves. Experts in business and psychology agree that creativity leads to innovation, and innovation leads to progress.

Time and again, we have witnessed yesterday's nonsense become today's reality. It wasn't so long ago that traveling to the moon and nuclear powered submarines were just figments in the minds of creative science fiction writers. Perhaps no one's creativity has had a greater impact on mankind than Johannes Gutenberg's. Combining two unrelated machines—a wine press and a coin punch—Gutenberg's creativity led to the printing press and moveable type.

Will the nonsense your children create in their imaginations become the seeds that generate presently unknown gifts to mankind? Unless you help your children develop and express that creativity, you—and the rest of the world—will never know.

much like those in this book) to reconnect with their creative selves—creative selves quashed by our hectic, workaday, media-saturated lives.

Creativity is necessary in all professions, all walks of life: As child development expert Cynthia MacGregor put it, "Creativity is an everyday necessity... it's important no matter what your aspirations for your child are, no matter what his interests or eventual career choices may be."

As parents, we have a wonderful opportunity to assist our children from the beginning. As more and more emphasis is placed on creativity as an important factor for success, parents may find that developing a child's creativity is the most "down to earth" training a child can receive. Nurture the creative spirit properly in the developing years, and actively teach creativity to older children, and you will help to raise adults who are successful in their work and their lives.

Many parents, however, have a hard time believing that they really can teach children to be more creative. Creativity seems so exotic. Many of us don't *feel* creative most of the time, so how can we teach it to others? And besides, isn't creativity just something you are born with? Can I really teach it to my child—like geography or math?

The answer to all these questions is YES, except that teaching creativity is a lot easier and often more fun than standard geography and math.

Yes, creativity is something we are born with—and we are all born with some of it. And a good thing, too.

The human species depends upon creativity for its survival. Just think for a moment of the numerous challenges, big and small, that you face every day, challenges that require you to think creatively. You probably were creative several times today.

It's precisely because all people, and especially children, have some creativity that you, the parent, can "teach" it. In this case teaching really just means exercising and encouraging your children's inborn creative ability. (That's why it is easier to teach creativity than geography or math.)

How do you teach a child sports? By encouraging her to practice her natural physical abilities, combined with some effective techniques. And put a big double line under *encouraging*—because that's more than half the battle.

> **Companies are now teaching grown-ups to reconnect with their creative selves.**

Of course, with very young children we don't actually tell them we are doing this. We don't announce, "It's time to practice."

Instead we encourage children to develop their physical, mental, and perceptual abilities by giving them the chance to do what comes naturally, through play.

Play is a great teacher. With play you never have to nag a child to do his homework. Play is also a fabulous way to interact with your child substantively—and enjoyably!—every day.

Play is crucial not only to humans but also to most higher species. Almost all mammals play, especially as infants. If they did not, they would never develop the abilities they need to survive.

That's how we teach creativity, too: by turning play into learning. The games and activities in this book encourage children to develop by doing what comes naturally.

And most important, this book will help you and your child to be creative *together*.

We talk to lots of busy parents, many who work outside the home, but many who are home as well. And busy parents (are there any nonbusy parents in our stressed-out era?) almost all tell us the same thing: "Sure I wish I could spend more time with my children, but I especially wish we could spend *better* time together."

Have you ever had this experience? It's the end of the day. Maybe you have just come home from work, or your child has just come home from day care. You ask her about what she did all day, hoping to share in the wonderful process of growing up. And you get a total of five words in response: "Yes," "No," and "I don't know." And you feel like a stranger. Or a failure.

You're not. It's just that your child needs help playing one of the most creative of all games, the language game.

This book will help. The games and exercises will help you share and shape your child's world, his thoughts and feelings, and will help him share them with you.

Because our approach is one of easy, creative play, much of it together, you will have more to talk about, and more of that "quality time" we are all hoping for. The language and imagination games especially will help make those one-word conversations a lot less frequent.

Years of research have identified the four basic traits of creative people, and using this knowledge, we can encourage creative development in children by playing some simple games that encourage those traits.

Experts agree that adults can contribute mightily to a child's creative development by encouraging her to observe, play with, and experiment with her environment. Many experts, including notable psychologists Jean Piaget and Jerome Bruner, argue that providing such opportunities is one of the most valuable things a parent can do for a child.

That is precisely what this book teaches you to do. Not through set formulas or exact procedures, but through playing with your child and showing her some games and activities she can do on her own.

These games and activities give children practice in the basic skills of creativity, but they do even more.

They encourage children to use their creativity rather than suppress it. They teach children that it is good to be creative and that creativity is a happy thing, something to be celebrated.

Research has also shown that one of the biggest factors in successful, creative, productive people is that they *believe* they can solve problems creatively and that they believe they can make change for the better.

The games in this book teach children to rejoice in their creativity, and teach you to rejoice with them.

Your children will be happier, more confident, and more productive. And you will be a happier parent, one who knows his children even better.

For creativity not only helps us survive, it also enhances all the lives it touches. Think of the joy of a creative moment and the added joy of creativity being expressed, shared, and appreciated. Then think of the joy and enrichment that come to you and your child from sharing such experiences together. Creative children are happy children. The more consistently their creativity is encouraged throughout their developmental years, the more creative they will be as they grow older.

This book will teach you how to encourage the natural creativity of a young child as well as improve the sagging creativity of an older child. Successfully fostering and nurturing creativity in children is part attitude, part strategy, and part love. But it also depends upon having a clear understanding of what creative behavior is.

In the following pages, you will learn how to recognize creative behavior and how to encourage such behavior in your children. Sometimes the results will be subtle, at other times dramatic.

It isn't difficult. And it's fun. After all, children are inherently creative. They are born with an innate drive to express new thoughts, to try new approaches, to ask unexpected questions. They want to be creative. This book will help you help them do what comes naturally.

> Playing with your child will not only enhance her creativity but will also increase the "quality time" you two spend together.

Because they are new to the world, children bring a fresh perspective to everything they look at, touch, listen to, and taste. They notice what we as adults have long since learned to ignore: the shapes of clouds, the sound of rain on a car roof, the springy texture of grass. It is all new information to them, and they use it in new ways.

The skills and capacities of small children expand day by day. When you sense your powers are growing, you try things, you experiment—and maybe you discover something new. Imagine a toddler using a stepstool. One day, he realizes it can move, then he realizes he is strong enough to move it, then he realizes he can move it up against the kitchen counter upon which rests the cookie jar! There: a young child creatively discovers how to get a snack for himself. Whether you want him to have this ability is another story, but the creative impulse is undeniable.

To encourage our children's natural creativity or to teach them how to be more creative, we must reacquaint ourselves with what creativity is. So in the next chapter we will start

with a solid working definition of creativity, based on a consensus of experts from many fields. In that chapter, you will
also learn

☆ the four basic behaviors shared by creative people;

☆ the important relationship between imagination and creativity; and

☆ the crucial distinction between creativity and lack of discipline in children.

In Chapters 3 and 4 you will learn just a bit more about how
to use play as a tool in child development, and how to nurture
creativity by working on your own attitudes as parents and fostering a household environment that encourages creativity.

Then in the next several chapters you'll learn about the
hands-on tools and techniques you will use to promote creativity in your children—the games and activities by which you
encourage creative play. These are arranged by both age and
activity type for easy use and reference.

The book will conclude with short chapters on how to evaluate two important influences in your children's lives and use
them to your benefit. The first is what we call the Media
Menagerie—the barrage of images, stories, characters, and
sounds that entertain us and our children but that also, if
allowed to play too big a role in our lives, distract and desen-
sitize developing minds.

The other important influence on children as they develop is,
of course, school. In Chapter 10, you'll get the answers to questions such as, Can a school nurture creativity? And how can
you evaluate your children's schools?

We conclude with a chapter called "Creative for Life,"
which discusses the link between a creative childhood and a

fulfilling, productive adult life. It's fun to realize that the activities you share with your kids when they're little can genuinely have a positive impact on their lives—and yours!

Just remember, it's fun, it comes naturally, and it's a lot easier than the new math! So let's begin.

CHAPTER TWO

What is Creativity?

"Any activity becomes creative when the doer cares about doing it right, or better."
—JOHN UPDIKE

A five-year-old becomes a king by wearing an old maroon bathrobe and a construction-paper crown. Young siblings turn a tale from their favorite story book into a theatrical presentation in the playroom. A toddler gathers acorns in a plastic bucket and "feeds" them to his stuffed bear. A preschooler plays airport with a pillow and a paper-towel tube—somehow.

From the far-fetched to the realistic and back again, childhood creativity is a many-splendored thing. As parents, we hear the word "creative" and tend to think "arts and crafts," but that's just an uncreative adult perspective. You don't need to be anywhere near paints, crayons, scissors, or glue to be creative, and you don't have to throw all those items in front of your kids to provide them with a creativity-enhancing experience.

So what is creativity? For our purposes in this book, creativity has a four-step definition:

1) the desire to IMPROVE things;

2) the tendency to undertake such improvements by looking at situations from a new point of view or REDEFINING a problem;

3) being OPEN to many new ideas or possible solutions, even those that seem "all wrong" at first; and then

4) ACTING on those fresh perspectives to CREATE novel solutions.

A tall order for a two-year-old? Not really. Two-year-olds do this all the time; in fact they do it more often than adults. They must, since the world is so new to them. They don't invent the helicopter, or split the atom. But as they learn to cope with the world they repeatedly act in the way creative people do. Those are the habits we want to encourage.

What Creativity is Not

- Creativity is not a product, a particular end result, or the "right" answer. It is a process of thinking and doing, a particular way of approaching life itself.
- Creativity is not genius or even talent. Unusually gifted individuals often display marvelous creativity. But you don't have to be a genius to be creative. You are creative when you can respond inventively, not just when you create a brilliant invention.
- Creativity is not magic or a mystical process, inaccessible to most mere mortals. Our brains were designed for creativity. Don't confuse the seeming magic of a brilliant creative idea (which probably took years of real totally unmagical work to develop) with the learned ability to approach life creatively.

So let's look at our definition again and change it into a more useful form: a description of how a creative person acts. When you understand that, it becomes easier to see how to nurture creativity not only in theory but also in practice.

Child psychologists, educators, historians, management gurus, and a host of experts looking at the subject of creativity have come up with a remarkably consistent list of four traits that creative people share. Even better, these four traits turn out to be mutually supportive so that encouraging one or several helps to build the others as well.

1. Creative people almost always display a desire, even a need, to improve things. Equally important, they have the self-esteem to know that they can, in fact, make things better.

This is an extremely important trait in creative people. One "historian of creativity" has pointed out that many of the greatest creative minds had a clear sense that they wished to change the world *and* the overwhelming belief that they could do so. Newton promised that he would "demonstrate the frame of the System of the World." Darwin thought of his work as setting forth "the Laws of Life." Even Einstein, known for his modesty, "clearly saw himself as the person whose thinking would transform physics." Researchers into creativity have spoken of the "courage to create" or noted that the most creative people see the gap between "what is" and "what could be," and believe that it is their personal mission to close that gap.

Of course, as other researchers into creativity have observed, if you want to "make things right," by definition you are starting from the assumption that something is wrong, or at least not as good as it could be. In other words, you are willing to challenge the status quo, to be a little different, or at least to consider the possibility. That leads right to our next two characteristics.

2. A creative individual has the ability to "think outside the box"—to see things from a unique perspective. When creative people are at work, common objects find unexpected uses, everyday tasks are accomplished in unanticipated ways, and accepted rules and conventional wisdom are questioned.

As we mentioned in Chapter 1, that's what Sikorsky did when he invented the helicopter; it was his new approach to the old question of how long airplane runways had to be. He completely redefined the terms of the problem.

This trait is one reason why being "good in school" does not necessarily mean that a child is creative. Tests largely measure the ability to think exactly as one has been taught to think. To the contrary, originality, unusual associations of ideas, and asking questions are essential to creativity. This is what researcher Patricia Haensly calls "testing the limits" and "daring to be different."

Sometimes extremely creative children can be so fond of "testing the limits" that they can be a real handful for parents and teachers. We'll discuss a bit later how to balance between allowing children the nonconformity they need to be creative and instilling self-discipline and a proper respect for others. But keep this in mind: Bad behavior is not creativity. The myth that all creative people are weird nonconformists who can't balance their checkbooks or stay out of trouble is just that—a myth. Creative people challenge the status quo by creating, not by being nuisances. In most cases even creative geniuses lead quite conventional lives.

3. A creative person keeps an open mind when challenged with new ideas, especially with absurd or unusual ones. Regardless of

how absurd or unusual such ideas might initially seem, a creative person rejects them only after honest and fresh consideration.

This is a big one. Almost all studies show that highly creative people *allow themselves* to have lots and lots of ideas. Most of those ideas are discarded. But creative people don't discard their new ideas just because they are new or because others don't share them. They give their new ideas at least a little bit of a chance. And they let their ideas grow, change, expand, and interact with other ideas.

Here is a simple example. Let's say your family is trying to decide where to take a family vacation. You get everyone around the table, and they start making suggestions. A lot of them are silly. Do

> Why do many children lose touch with their creative selves as they grow?

you say no to the silly ones right away, or do you add them to the list, and only take them off later when the list is very long and it is time to choose? The second way is the way the creative person's mind works. He always has lots of ideas to choose from because he is not afraid or embarrassed to experiment.

The research into creativity and creative children and adults is unanimous on this point. Some experts talk about "fluency" or "ideaphoria," the production of many ideas as a basic skill of the creative. Psychologists have observed that creative people tend to have relatively low needs for "repression" or "suppression" as defense mechanisms. Creative people allow themselves more images, ideas, and information to work with when they are solving a problem.

4. Creative people are driven by the need to implement their ideas. They not only see ways to improve a situation, they also make the improvements happen. Many people believe that "ideas" or "imagination" lie at the heart of creativity. But

unless the ideas are implemented nothing is created. As educational psychologist Joseph S. Renzulli notes, the creative individual is willing to take risks, not just in thought but in action. Most of us can develop a dozen ideas before breakfast on how to organize road repair schedules more efficiently, run the country more competently, or eliminate world starvation. It's easy because we don't have to test our ideas against reality. Our "creative" ideas might all be nonsense (and probably are). And untested nonsense is nothing more than daydreaming. Even a fine idea, if unimplemented, is of as little value as a radio broadcast to a deserted island.

Virtually all the great creative people of history were known not as dreamers but as hard workers, with great perseverance. One reason creativity is not the same as intelligence or IQ is that a high IQ person with no drive to make his ideas into reality rarely does much creative work.

Fortunately, this drive to turn ideas into reality tends to come naturally to people who have the other three traits, and vice versa. As Renzulli points out, "creativity and task commitment almost always stimulate each other." When a person has a creative idea he is more than likely to decide to do something with it and thus he develops the commitment to action. By the same token, a person committed to getting a job done will often be stimulated to have creative ideas on how to do it.

Your mother knew a simpler way to say this: "Necessity is the mother of invention."

These four behaviors form the basis for creativity in adults. But notice the wonderful thing about all four of them: All are behaviors that we can easily encourage in children.

In fact, as we'll see, teaching your child creativity really comes down to just two things:

1. Helping to give her LOTS of opportunities to practice these four behaviors and turn them into habits. That's where the games and activities in this book come in.

2. Being VERY encouraging about all four of these behaviors so your child knows you approve, and associates these behaviors with happy, exciting times. This includes creating a home environment in which these four behaviors are practiced and valued by adults as well as children.

> As a parent, you can start encouraging creativity today.

Once we understand what creative people have in common, it is easy to see that a huge part of the job of nurturing creativity in young children simply comes down to encouraging freedom of expression—allowing their naturally uninhibited natures to flourish through play, song, dance, and simple crafts. And by no means does it all have to happen through structured activities.

Consider a two-year-old's delight in the raspberry (not the fruit—the mouth noise). Babies usually learn to imitate this satisfying sound while lying on the changing table at some point, but it's the toddler who can turn it into a gleeful highlight of the day. You make a raspberry; he makes a raspberry. He giggles. He makes it again, more assertively. More giggling.

Okay, nothing creative is happening—yet. So far he is only copying you. So the next time, you change it—maybe by shaking your head or wiggling your shoulders. Maybe he'll copy you again. But eventually he will probably make one for you that's a bit different. Maybe now you begin responding to his efforts with elaborate body language of your own—you jump in the air, hide your face, spin around, and so forth.

Maybe he'll imitate you, but he probably will begin to try his own raspberry experiments. And the first time he doesn't follow you, but does something deliberately different (scrunches down after you have jumped up?), he'll probably seem extra pleased with himself—as if he has just made the biggest joke in the world.

He is no longer imitating you. Rather, *he is imitating the process of making changes.* In so doing, he is making creative changes of his own. Before you know it, his raspberry involves dancing or stomping or maybe even a whole lot of extra saliva.

A toddler making a raspberry while doing a little jig is, in a way, acting out all four creativity behaviors at once: he is *improving* on the original raspberry; he is approaching a mouth noise from a *new perspective* (adding body movement); he is approaching the whole endeavor and adding these new

---

Not Just Art

There is no denying the creative power of art and the creative spirit of the artist. But the arts do not have a monopoly on creativity.

Resist the urge to assume that art supplies have to be used whenever you're seeking a creativity-enhancing experience. Because creativity involves a well-developed imagination and an open-minded approach to the world, a lot of what you can do to encourage creativity in your kids requires no supplies beyond your time and attention.

Even so, most experts still believe that the arts are central to developing creativity in children and that they provide a tremendously fulfilling way for growing children to express their feelings nonverbally. What parents should understand is that artistic expression is every child's birthright, as the box entitled "'Creativity' is Not 'Talent'" demonstrates.

developments *without any judgment* whatsoever; and he is certainly *getting the job done!*

And yet he is too young to be told this. (And a good thing, too. The last thing we want to let the happy infant know is that he is doing creativity "lessons" and they are "for his own good.")

Likewise he is too young to be expected to display more "mature" creativity. Thank goodness there is no right way to do a raspberry, and no way for people to tell him his raspberry is wrong.

Marvelously, all you have to do to nurture creativity is to encourage his joy and delight in creative expression. Your child will be all the more ready to respond later to more-developed creativity-enhancing "techniques" if joyful expression of them is encouraged at an early age.

Creativity requires that the mind be at its imaginative best, and imagination is, by its nature, a free-flowing, unpredictable entity. And it is joyful. You might want to think of creativity as the process by which human beings experience life's wonders in the most personal way.

Our raspberrying toddler may not be the picture of social decorum, but he's as happy with himself at that moment as most adults could ever wish to be. The more joy and creative expression are linked in a young child, and the more encouragement he receives regarding such behavior, the more likely he will be to accept being taught creativity later on. And the more creative a person he will become.

And remember, encouragement is crucial. One wonderful thing about encouragement is that it begins at home. As a parent, you can start today, as soon as you put down this book, to adopt a more encouraging attitude to creativity with your child. The impact will be clear and continual. And because much of the play in this book is "talking play," in teaching your child creativity you can foster communication with your child.

Creativity Lost

Now let's compare the toddler's delight in the raspberry to the reaction an older child might have to one of life's little wonders. Imagine you're walking into the house with your twelve-year-old one evening and notice a lovely sliver of the moon in the sky. "Ooh, look at the moon," you might say. "Uh huh," she might reply.

How does a toddler who rollicks in the creative joy of physical expression become a sullen, wonder-less pre-adolescent? How does an action-oriented three-year-old—who wants an item and grabs for it—become a procrastinating couch potato in her teenage years? There is little question that many children lose touch with their creative selves as they grow. But why does this happen?

Well, sometimes day-to-day reality just doesn't seem to have a place for the creative spirit that all children have from birth. Other times, a child's creativity is ignored. Children have such remarkable inborn creativity that parents sometimes take it for granted without even realizing it. At other times, while teaching necessary rules of behavior, parents trample creativity to death. They don't mean to. But because they don't think "Oh, she is being creative now," they may miss a chance to encourage or nurture creativity. They may even send the message that creativity is unwelcome.

"Now wait a second," you might say. "When my child is being creative, I notice her." And you do—most of the time. But creativity can be easy to overlook—precisely because it is so natural.

To take just one example, it's safe to say that one of the most astonishing feats of inborn creativity a child demonstrates is almost completely unappreciated. This is the process of learning language. Of course, we fuss and cheer when our eleven-month-old first points to her mother and says "ma-ma," but we often overlook the real creativity of the process.

Think about it: the overwhelming majority of sentences anyone hears and speaks in his or her lifetime are new! And yet, somehow, our brains understand what is said to us and easily produce new sentences to meet the requirements of life as it unfolds moment by moment. A child learning language expresses a desire to change and improve her situation almost moment by moment—and instantly implements those changes.

> You and your child can develop a wonderful relationship through creative play.

Even creativity experts don't always recognize this sort of creativity because it becomes so entangled with linguistic rules and structure. Nevertheless, there is a sign of innate human creativity here if you look for it. And if you're on your toes as a parent, you can sometimes pinpoint milestones in the process.

I remember a day when my first son, at twenty-two months, had lost track of his stuffed bunny. "Bunny go," he was saying as he shuffled around the house. This was his way of asking where the bunny had gone. I realized it was in the car and told him so. He thought for a moment, then looked me in the eye and said, with endearing toddler inflection, "Go get it."

It was the beginning of a never-ending series of commands he would give. But at the time it seemed startling; the newness of this sentence-producing power created a look on his face that was both puzzled and proud. He's nine now, but I still remember this clearly.

How do we miss the signs of creativity? The very things that make children naturally creative are the things that make so many of us, as adults, struggle with creativity. As we move from childhood into adolescence, young adulthood, and beyond, we are no longer new to the world. Our skills and capabilities are no longer growing daily. Our inhibitions are.

We may ourselves remain very creative: in our jobs, even at home and at play (if we have any time for play).

But because we are so far from childhood we may not recognize in our children those creative moments that are not only helping him develop now but, depending in part on our reactions, also may be helping to build the creative habits of a lifetime.

That's why in order to help our children to be creative, we should think just a bit more about the way a child grows and develops. Let's do that next.

"Creativity" is Not "Talent"

Many of us think that a creative person is a sort of talented specialist. For example, "artists" create art, which hangs in galleries and museums. "Musicians" write or perform music for concert halls and compact discs.

It is time we re-embraced a more generalized definition of creativity. Everyone is born with a creative instinct, and creativity should not be judged by anyone's standard. Children lacking artistic or musical talent are not necessarily lacking in creativity. With young children in particular, it's the act of expression that must be encouraged and treasured, not the level of aesthetic achievement. As children become older, their grasp of the creative mindset will help them grow into truly creative adults, regardless of how "artistic" they are.

CHAPTER THREE

Learning Through Play

"The creative individual. . . is capable of questioning the assumptions that the rest of us accept."
—JOHN W. GARDNER

Improving your child's creativity is not only easy, it's actually fun. Your efforts will be rewarded many times over as you witness the expansion of your child's mind as well as the flowering of your own relationship.

Encouraging your child's creativity is fun because play is at the heart of the process. But we must carefully define play, because not all play is creative play. A six-year-old running his toy cars around on their track is having fun, but he is not necessarily being creative. He is doing merely what the instructions that came with the toy say he ought to do.

Of course he may be being creative in his own mind—making up stories about who is in the cars and how the big race is going. And if the child eventually moves the cars off the track and pretends they can fly, you can be sure he has entered the realm of creative play.

It is through play that a child's creativity is most fully and frequently expressed. Carl Jung wrote that "the dynamic principle of fantasy is play, which... appears to be inconsistent with the principle of serious work. But without this playing with fantasy, no creative work has ever yet come to birth."

Play is fundamental to creativity. And play is fundamental to child development; in fact it is one of the most powerful forces in this development. Children spend, and for their own good must spend, an enormous portion of their time in play. It is through directing play (subtly, of course) that you can have the greatest influence on your child's creativity.

> Play is fundamental to creativity and to child development.

To begin to understand the importance of play, it is useful to recognize that children and adults think differently. These differences are generic; that is, children *as a group* think differently from adults *as a group*. So, although adults who are considered "childish" by their peers may exhibit some of the thought characteristics of children, their thought processes are in fact very different.

There are four primary differences between the thinking of children and that of adults:

1. *Logical thinking:* Adults have been taught to consider alternatives and then to reject those that don't seem logical; children, by contrast, have not yet learned the process of rejecting the illogical. To understand this distinction more clearly, consider the way we as adults think: As soon as one thought is set in our mind, we move onto the next one and then pause momentarily to see whether it "fits" logically with the first thought. If it does, we move onto the third thought. Otherwise, we reject the second thought and then search for an alternative. In other words, our thoughts need to "make sense." Of course, such a logical thought process can inhibit creativity by cutting off flights of fancy before they start. As

creative adults we have to make an effort to temporarily "suspend our disbelief."

Now think about children. They can move on to a second thought even if it bears little relationship to the first one. Little children often jump from one thought to the next without a logical connection, so their thoughts often sound like nonsense to adults. There certainly is a creative spark present in this type of thinking, but most of these illogical thoughts will ultimately prove impractical.

That is where play comes in. Play fosters *useful* creative thinking in children. While playing, children develop the logic process as an overlay to the original creative spark inherent in their "illogical" thought. Playing forces some rules onto children without inhibiting their imagination. For instance, if a child comes up with the grand "creative" idea of building a pyramid made of marbles, he'll quickly discover that, because marbles roll by nature, the pyramid just isn't likely to work!

2. *Prior knowledge and the imagination:* Because children have far less prior knowledge than adults, their imaginations have much more room to flourish. A child can, for instance, imagine a table as a tent far more easily than an adult can, simply because she is not yet inhibited by the information that tents are made of canvas and have walls that touch the ground.

Many of us have had the experience of reading to young children. If we accidentally skip a page, the child will often be quite happy to continue the story in spite of the gap. The resulting logic lapse doesn't bother the child nearly as much as it bothers the adult reader because the child simply hasn't learned that story lines must flow in a logical progression.

Certainly, the lack of factual burdens can help the child's imagination, but facts must be added into the equation of creativity as the child grows. Play is an excellent way of letting children absorb factual information without inhibiting their creativity. Think of the pyramid of marbles again: a child trying this will certainly acquire knowledge about the "facts" of marbles!

3. *Freedom from embarrassment:* Since young children do not yet understand the logic process, they are not embarrassed by logical mistakes. This means that they can think almost anything they like. There is little political correctness, far less "what will others think." Just imagine what it would be like if we, as adults, could think anything we like—and express it—without fear of making a bad impression or in some other way embarrassing ourselves. What extraordinary freedom we would have!

Of course, even very young children can be embarrassed, especially around peers, and so even at an early age conformity comes into play. A friend of ours described how, when his sister began preschool, she and the other children were asked to draw carrots. The girl had a great natural ability to draw objects realistically, just as she saw them. So she began to draw a quite recognizable carrot. But then she looked at a large orange smudge the boy sitting next to her had drawn as his "carrot." She threw away her realistic drawing and copied the boy's smudge.

In other words, our children will eventually have to deal with the limitations the world places upon us all. And playing is a great way to introduce your child to those unavoidable limitations. When playing with your child, you can show her that making mistakes is "no big deal." So, during a game you can *gently* introduce your child to the concept of needing "correct" factual underpinnings.

4. *Differing objectives:* Children and adults often have fundamentally different *objectives* of thought. Adults think mostly in order to reach a conclusion, to make a decision and then implement it. Children, on the other hand, think largely for pleasure and for the exercise of their imaginations, and so they are much less results-oriented than their parents. They think, imagine, and indulge in flights of fancy, just for the sheer joy of it.

Consider the thoughts you have every day: what to cook for dinner, whether you can afford a new car, where the dog might be. Children aren't as bound by the need to think to reach decisions. If they think of the dog at all, it is more likely to be to wonder what would happen if it could fly. And their thoughts about a new car end with "I want one"—which is where their parents' thinking starts!

Since play—and particularly imaginative play—is largely based on thought without consequence, it fits particularly well into children's mode of thinking. But, since some consequences do exist even for play, play helps maintain the child's creativity within the parameters of responsible decision making, implementation, and action.

There are nearly as many theories of play as there are theorists, but whatever their perspective, researchers agree that different types of play are essential at different points in the developmental process. You do not need to be a child psychologist to know that a six-year-old approaches the world very differently than a two-year-old does. You see that she talks differently, moves differently, plays differently, finds different things funny, and engages in her activities in completely different ways.

For this reason knowing a little about children's developmental stages can help you foster your child's creativity. This will help you guide your child's creative play in an age-appropriate way. Interacting with younger children is substantively different from approaching older children, even if the goal is the same.

Younger children are generally more naturally attuned to their creative instincts than older children. It is important, however, to know what children are capable of learning and when, both cognitively and emotionally. Finally, because creativity manifests itself differently in small children than in older children or adults, it must be nurtured somewhat differently, too.

Knowing a bit about the stages of development can serve you well in three ways:

⚝ *Choosing activities:* You will be better able to choose which creative activities are likely to appeal to your child.

⚝ *Setting expectations:* You will have a better understanding of how your child will participate in a given activity.

⚝ *Guiding the interaction:* You will see how you as a parent can steer your child through an activity—what you might say to get him interested, what you might ask to launch his imagination, when to step back and let him continue on his own.

It has been suggested that children progress through a series of four distinct development phases, each of which can be seen in different types of play:

⚝ Learning through trial and error (ages 0 to 2)—As a child gains motor control, he begins to sense his own boundaries and learns to use simple tools. The raspberry game (see Chapter 2) is a good example.

✿ Learning by pretending (ages 2 to 7)—Pretend play flourishes and grows more sophisticated, as does a child's ability to express herself verbally.

✿ Playing by the rules (ages 7 to 11)—Pretend play is gradually phased out and replaced by the social conventions of mutually agreed upon rules.

✿ Games that require deductive reasoning à la Sherlock Holmes (ages 11 to 15)—Adolescents gain the ability to think in an abstract manner, the ability to combine and classify items in a more sophisticated way, and the capacity for higher-order reasoning.

During these four phases, a child becomes consistently better able to deal with the abstract. Purely physical experience is replaced with thought, and each stage represents a qualitative, irreversible advance over the previous stage.

As Swiss psychologist Jean Piaget has stated, "What is desired is that the teacher cease being a lecturer, satisfied with transmitting ready-made solutions; his role should rather be that of a mentor stimulating initiative and research."

Infants and Toddlers

Child psychologist Penelope Leach says, "If you provide playthings for fun, your child will educate herself. If you buy toys for education, she will not always have fun." Neither, therefore, will she learn very much. That is why the best "educational toys" are always created to be fun first, and educational only as a huge fringe benefit—unrecognized by the child.

While Leach made the comment regarding babies, it spreads beyond the first two years of a child's life. As a parent, it's worth reminding yourself that through the preschool years, at the very least, your child learns without trying to learn; he learns simply by being.

Almost everything the new child does is educational or at least developmental, and most of it can be thought of as a form of play.

With two- and three-year-olds in particular, to guide their play creatively you'll need to spend a lot of time acting silly. Many activities for children this age involve playing with their new-found motor control; the more you can throw yourself into the action, the greater the joy you'll see in your child. There's nothing like the spark in a two-and-a-half-year-old's eyes when she watches Mommy whirling and hopping around to music. The child almost always responds with new ideas of her own. At this age, your child is learning not only to copy your specific behavior, but your willingness to be unconventional. Your child is starting to emulate being creative.

> Fostering creativity is one of the most lasting gifts you can give your child.

Remember that at this stage of development, creativity is expressed with naive simplicity. A three-year-old who decides, while listening to music, to slap his thigh after each hop is being creative if he's never seen that move before. Some children at this age may engage in even more unexpected moves—picking up a nearby book or stuffed animal, for instance, and adding it to the activity. The less you show him specifically what to do and the more you show your happiness and appreciation, the more you are using the activity to enhance creativity.

While most activities you set up for two- or three-year-olds to nurture creativity will involve a fair amount of parental interaction, don't forget to allow your toddler private space for some solo play time. Children this age need time apart—to process and respond to the deluge of information they constantly receive and the emotions it evokes, as well as simply to begin to nudge themselves toward autonomy. Activities in which toddlers can either be left alone or allowed to operate without guidance or interpretation from you almost always encourage creativity.

When it comes to introducing the sorts of activities you'll find in Chapter 5, remember that toddlers appreciate a choice. Without a choice, children this age often exhibit the charming habit of refusing something offered to them—even a favorite toy or dessert—simply because it was foisted upon them rather than chosen by them.

One Step Up

As three-year-olds become four-year-olds, small motor skills improve and activities can involve more close work (manipulating small objects, for example). Also, social skills advance enough to allow meaningful group play and even participation in formal games. But imagination is still what lies at the center of the children's play world. To young preschoolers, just about everything they learn and every emotion they experience feed into their make-believe world.

When you guide your three- or four-year-old through creative activities involving imagination, resist the urge to impose some sort of logic on the proceedings. Child psychologists advocate taking the role of active listener rather than overt guide. Provide the settings; the child will contribute the action.

Children derive great pleasure from creating and controlling a world entirely their own—a world in which they decide what goes where and what happens when.

Of course, not all fantasies are totally original. Some are simply ways of expressing new perspectives. Thus, a child given an electronic board game with pictures of various animals and buttons that make the appropriate animal sound may first choose the "right" button—"moo" for the cow, "baaa" for the lamb. But then, with tremendous gurgling delight, he may purposely pretend that a cow says "baaa." The parent's response, "What a funny cow that is!"—accompanied of course by lots of laughter—causes much more delight than would even the most gently worded correction. By joining the game, the adult tells the child that it's okay to consider even absurd alternatives, which is the very essence of creativity.

By contrast, correcting the child would teach him nothing new about the sounds animals make; the child understood that idea long ago. Instead, it teaches that you get praised only if you stick to the rules, i.e., creativity's antithesis.

The point here is that this part of a childhood phase can become a lifetime capability, thanks to your parental role as encourager and enabler. Divergent thinking (another term for that heavy flow of unusual ideas that creative people have) is, after all, the very cornerstone of adult creativity.

Think back to the four characteristics of creative individuals: wanting to improve things, seeing things from a unique perspective, keeping an open mind to new ideas, and taking action. These attitudes are most easily generated in a child who has from an early age been given both the time and encouragement to play and fantasize freely.

Beyond overtly encouraging creative fantasy play, parents can foster creativity in their preschoolers by supporting specific play interests as they emerge. Be careful, however, to avoid pigeonholing a child. The goal here is neither to create nor to break patterns, but to allow children to experience the joyfulness of a beloved activity. Some creativity experts assert that these experiences can deepen and enrich a developing imagination. There is little better food for the imagination than complete absorption in a joyful activity. From the age of about four onward, such a state is increasingly possible for children. But, again, be careful, for the opposite can apply: there is little that stymies creative joy more effectively than always having to play within the rules.

Another important piece of the creativity puzzle at this age is art in general, and drawing in particular. Pablo Picasso, who kept toys in his studio as inspiration, once remarked, "Every child is an artist. The problem is how to remain an artist once he grows up."

Activities involving drawing are an especially good idea for this age group, especially when bolstered by the creativity-enhancing attitudes we will describe in more detail in the chapters ahead. Setting up an art table is a nice way to begin. It doesn't take much—a stack of blank paper, some construction paper, and some markers are a fine start. Depending on your tolerance for having scraps of paper on the floor, you might throw in some scissors, tape, and a glue stick as well. Crayons, of course, are good, but they're more attractive to your child if they're organized in a box rather than tossed in a bucket of worn-out looking scraps. Colored pencils can be nice as a change of pace.

The idea of the art table is that it's always there, always reasonably neat, and always well stocked so that it invites your child to sit and create something. Keep a small trash can nearby for throwing out scraps and unwanted paper. As much as you want to encourage your child to clean up after herself, help her straighten up the table if she's worked hard. As certainly as children seem to like making a mess, they also begin to steer clear of the messes they've made, to find other places to play.

Not everyone may have the space to create an art table. An alternative is to put together a well-stocked, portable box that contains all the aforementioned supplies. This can be your child's "art box," which is always kept handy for use in the same way as the art table. Again, the key here is helping your child keep the box neat; too disheveled an art box will be a box that is too soon stashed away and forgotten in a closet.

> Nurturing creativity is within the power of all parents—even those who work full-time.

The art table is a perfect example of how you can nurture your child's creativity—even at those times when you're not intimately involved in their play. Many children lose the originality and expressive capability of their preschool age when they enter school and begin to observe and emulate more conventional styles; the longer we can keep our children in touch with their natural expressive instincts, the more we nourish their creative spirits.

School and Beyond

Imaginative play will begin to grow more orderly and logical of its own accord as your child matures. But the play will remain marked by odd and wonderful jumps into the purely fantastic. This is the special aspect of the play that should be encouraged in a creativity-friendly household. Encouragement can foster a young child's instinctive ability to view the world in unconventional ways and inspire him to continue using it as he grows older.

Fostering creativity through the school years is one of the most lasting gifts you can give your child—a gift that this book teaches you how to give. These are the years in which the conscientious teaching of the four behavioral precepts introduced in Chapter 2 can begin in earnest. Children of this age are old enough to understand what "conventional" is and why looking beyond it when thinking and playing can be both fun and rewarding.

But don't forget that children are developing physically as well as mentally. Even as kids venture further into the realm of complex thought and reasoning, they continue to learn best, and more enduringly, if they're able to absorb new concepts physically as well. "I hear and I forget. I see and I remember. I do and I understand," wrote the Chinese poet and philosopher Lao-tse. Activities that children cannot only see and hear but also touch and feel are wonderfully suited for most school-age kids.

It's a lesson to remember as your children move through elementary school and beyond. The imagination—that all-important wellspring of creativity—remains engaged through appeals to different senses, and hands-on activities become, if anything, even more important for older children who might otherwise lose touch with their expressive selves.

This is important to remember, because all too much of children's play today is anything but hands-on, and far from expressive.

Activities involving storytelling, as offered in Chapter 7, are ideally suited for children in this age group. With your child's communication skills improving continuously, the stories she tells will become better and better. And don't forget to include props. Acting out the stories will add the aspect of physicality that is so important.

Time for the Imagination

Creativity is nurtured by unstructured time. This is a thought worth pondering. Research indicates that free, unstructured, imaginative play not only encourages creativity but also contributes to language development and improves attention spans. As a culture, we are failing our children here in an extraordinary way. Extraordinary because we are acting, collectively, in direct opposition to the needs and natural interests of our children.

Unstructured time means open-ended time to become involved in a real life, three-dimensional, not very organized activity—time to allow the imagination to unfold, stretch its wings, and soar. To play without strict guidelines. Or merely to daydream.

The games and exercises in this book, while certainly more structured than daydreaming, help fulfill the child's need to let the imagination go.

Unfortunately much of what we call play today does just the opposite.

While a good television or computer program can encourage imaginative activities, a child's imagination is not itself exercised while in front of a screen. After all, a computer is a highly structured machine; most of the programs created for it quickly betray the equally highly structured nature of their design. Even so-called "interactive" computer programs rarely function in a creatively open-ended way.

Children hurried through a childhood structured as a series of organized activities—or in the case of computer games, organized inactivity—will grow up with their creativity impaired, and may also experience stress. They won't have a chance to think for themselves, to create. And they won't feel the need to make things happen for themselves: circumstances, not their own initiative, will rule their lives. It's our job as parents to realize this, even if it means opposing the social norm at times. Fortunately, it is within the power of all parents—even those who have to work full-time—to avoid this danger. Indeed, in some ways, working parents have an easier time of it than parents who are constantly at home. You see, kids do need structure—it is, after all, a condition of all our lives, and children have to learn to cope with it.

But they also need freedom from structure, freedom to create. With working parents, the two are easily differentiated; structure is provided by the institutions which take over when the parents are not present—the day-care center, the school, etc. Freedom to create is when Mommy and Daddy come home. It's fun time, freedom time, creativity time.

For parents who are at home most of the time, the differentiation is less clear cut. They set the rules most of the time. Thus, they have to work a little harder at also setting time aside when rules are less important... not ignored entirely, but less immediate—i.e., "creativity" time.

By nurturing our children's creativity, we provide our children with the potential for fulfilling and productive lives. In the next chapter we will get down to the practical business of doing precisely that.

CHAPTER FOUR

Getting Started

"It is in games that many men discover their paradise."
—ROBERT LYND

We are just about ready to begin.

To begin playing, that is. Because that's what this book is about—doing something you already do with your child, playing, but doing so in a way that also teaches the habits of creativity.

We'll spend much of the chapter talking about the games and exercises in this book, most of which are easy and many of which can be played anywhere—even in the car—without any materials.

But in addition to the specific games, it is important that you impart the spirit of creativity to your children, especially by example.

Once you learn how to do that, all your play with your children, and other times as well, can enhance their creativity, even if you are not using these games at all.

Because even though these specific games were designed to teach the four basic behaviors of creative people, we could have designed dozens of different games to do the same thing, or found other ways to introduce creativity into play—and so can you.

The real point is that this book will teach you how to guide your children into types of play that will improve their creativity. As you do so remember to avoid the appearance of structured learning. No attempt to improve creativity that also appears to restrict play will succeed. While it isn't necessary for you to enter completely into your child's play world, you need to understand how important it is in child development and in the development of the creative spirit, as the previous chapter showed.

Once you do, you'll hit upon a wonderful truth: striving to improve a child's creativity is not, and cannot be, work. The

> **Most of the games and activities are easy, and many can be played anywhere.**

minute it starts to feel like work, step back and question your motives and actions. Although it will sometimes take an effort, if it feels like work to you it will sound like work to your child and you will accomplish little. Children are not adults. Adults may need and even want consultants to help them improve their creativity. Most children learn grudgingly, if at all, when they feel someone is trying to control their behavior.

Keep yourself infused with a genuine spirit of play—even when challenging your children to push their minds in creative new directions—and creativity will flourish. Internalize the four basic creative behaviors you're attempting to nurture so that you don't sound as if you're constantly instructing your children.

Remember: The collection of specific games and activities is meant to be a *help* to you, not a test to see if you as a parent are doing it "right." Take them all as playful suggestions, not as a checklist you must work through.

The Creative Parent

You, the parent, are the true teacher. And you teach mostly by example. Let's think about that.

Improving your children's creativity begins with your attitude toward the world around you. Is it the attitude of a creative person, open to experience, really seeing the world around him afresh, to stimulate his understanding in new ways?

Cultivate the attitudes of creativity. Here are three ways to do that:

1. *Be mindful of your surroundings:* Really look at what you're seeing; really listen to what you're hearing. How often do you actually hear the birds singing outside when you're leaving the house? Did you ever notice the way your teapot shakes before it starts to boil? Neither of these things is an earth-shaking realization. But the point here is less the intrinsic value of the observation than the process of observing.

This awareness will help you see the world a bit more like your child does. Young children tend to be beautifully mindful, partly because everything is new to them. The more you can aim at this state of mind yourself, the more you can promote it in your child, especially as he moves into the age where it tends to slip away.

One way you can practice mindfulness is to make a point of drawing your child's attention to new things or ideas she has not yet recognized for herself. You can actually give yourself a goal: each day, point out perhaps two new observations to your child. Maybe on Day 1 you show her a new leaf sprouting from a seed and point out how some dogs don't have tails; on Day 2 you can comment on how an artificial fire log burns with colored flames and how boiling water creates steam. The list of new ideas is endless.

2. *Rekindle your sense of wonder:* This is another childlike state that adults tend to overlook. If you feel that perhaps you've lost your sense of awe, you can tune it up by remembering that it's okay to let go and think as inquisitively as you did when you were a child. If you really look at a star and think about all that it represents—its unfathomable heat, its incomprehensible mass, the way its mind-boggling distance reveals to us an image that literally takes us back in time—you will be able to rekindle your sense of childlike wonder. Your ability to communicate the endless wonder of the world to your children is an invaluable contribution to their developing creative spirits.

3. *Maintain a spirit of playfulness:* As the day progresses through its routine rhythms, be ready with a smile, a funny comment, an unexpected reaction. It can be the littlest thing. Perhaps your six-year-old comes home from school and asks for some pretzels, just as he does every day. Today you can smile and say, "Pretzels? Since when do you like pretzels?" Or break into a spontaneous song as you serve them. Yes, it's hard sometimes to conjure this mood after a stressful day, but just as the act of smiling actually improves your mood, so does the effort to project a playful disposition work to energize you. And creativity thrives in a playful house.

You may notice that many of the activities designed to help improve your child's creativity require a certain amount of "on the fly" creativity from you. If, for instance, you're taking your child on a tour of an art museum, you may have to say more than "Look at the pretty picture!"

Using the art museum visit as a concrete example, here are four quick tips to help you switch on your creativity so your child can, too.

☼ *Use silly substitutes:* Free-associate in your mind to conjure an unexpected word in an otherwise normal question or statement. In the museum, if you're looking at a painting of a woman holding an umbrella, you can ask, "What if that woman were holding a clarinet instead? Where would she be going?"

☼ *Concoct clever combinations:* Creativity is sometimes sparked simply by thinking of combining two things that are already in front of you. In the art museum, you might engage your child by saying you're going to combine two of the paintings into one, then have him create a story that would incorporate images from both.

☼ *Bend over backwards:* Look at the world upside down, literally. If, say, an abstract painting doesn't provoke any feelings or stories as it is, suggest that you both look at it upside down for a minute.

☼ *Break the rules!:* Creativity can flourish when life takes an unexpected turn—when, for instance, you announce that you and your child are going to take a walk in the pouring rain. Normally, of course, the rule is that you can't play in the rain. The unexpected activity is a natural creativity booster. In the art museum, of course, there are institutional rules that must be followed. But there may be family rules you can "break" to foster imaginative reactions.

For instance, you might not normally like your child to use a harsh word such as "ugly" about anyone else's artwork. But just for fun, do the unexpected and ask your child to choose the absolutely ugliest painting he sees and have him explain why it's ugly and how it makes him feel. He may even do something unexpected himself, such as asking when he can come back to the museum again.

So, if it sounds to you as if parents are also expected to live creatively, you're right. There's no better way to foster creativity. This doesn't mean you have to be able to draw or sing, spin elaborate tales, or concoct unusual inventions. Just show your kids that you like to try new things. That you appreciate new ideas. That you don't take conventional wisdom at face value. Let them see you acting silly, getting your hands dirty, inventing goofy songs, dancing to music on the radio.

Inspire Creativity

Beyond providing an example of creativity when you can, there are specific ways you can behave with your children that will nurture their creative spirits, both during creativity-oriented activities and while going about everyday life.

❈ *Be a good listener:* Nothing inspires people to expand their thinking and develop ideas more than the knowledge that someone is truly listening. When you talk with your child, avoid asking too many yes/no questions or "automatic" questions like, "How was school?" All you will probably get is the answer, "Okay, I guess."

To elicit information, you must use *concrete* questions. Ask your child, "Did Mr. McCarthy tell you about dinosaurs today?" You may get a quick yes. But then you could start the conversation rolling by asking an open-ended question like, "If you had a pet dinosaur, what would it look like?" Just thinking about the question will embark your child on a creative journey.

※ *Be patient:* Whenever possible, try not to rush your children, especially while they're talking or creating. Kids need more time than most adults realize when they are caught up in what they're doing. Do your best to respond to your child's rhythms, not to your own.

※ *Tolerate mess:* Creative activities are sometimes less than neat. Relax your aversion to disorder at least while you're in the middle of a creative activity. When you do, your children will feel freer to experiment and enjoy it.

※ *Inspire perseverance:* This book focuses on activities that show you how to foster creativity in your children. But be aware that if you introduce too many new activities to your children, they will become distracted, more interested in what's next than in what they're doing. Before you have them begin an activity, discuss it with excitement. Allow them to sense the potential of what they'll be doing.

Important: Curb your urge to take things over and do most of the activity for your children just to hurry them along. Remember that your goal is to encourage your children to persevere and create through the activity.

※ *Tolerate the offbeat:* Creativity comes in all shapes and sizes and marches to its own drummer. Children taught too early to suppress unusual ideas will find it less natural to innovate and brainstorm as they grow.

Creativity versus Acting Out

One more thought before we begin. We have said a great deal about the need to encourage free expression and being open to new ideas—about not limiting your child's sense of adventure.

But lest there be any misunderstanding: Finger-painting on the new carpet isn't "free expression."

And bouncing a ball off the neighbor's window to see if it makes a good handball court isn't "seeing things in a new perspective."

And teaching creativity doesn't mean letting your kids run wild. Or being a weak parent. In fact some research suggests that "strong" parents raise more creative children than weak or lax ones.

The freedom the creative spirit needs isn't perpetual unfetteredness or complete latitude. A child given too much freedom is just as liable to run into trouble as a child given too little.

The freedom the creative spirit thrives on is the freedom to think without limitations, the freedom to take initiative, the freedom to be spontaneous—the freedom, basically, to act freely, but within the loose but important boundaries of responsibility.

A sense of balance is one of the most important traits a parent can have, especially when encouraging creativity.

The line between a creative child and an undisciplined child may be a fine one at times, but it is usually clear. Still some parents sometimes have trouble discerning it. We all know parents who, for example, let their three-year-old answer the telephone. Or parents who let their six-year-old decide when he's going to bed.

It's one thing to treat your child with respect; it's another to allow a human being who doesn't know what's best for her or anyone else make decisions for which she is not developmentally prepared.

Similarly, it's one thing to encourage self-expression, another thing when that self-expression occurs without regard to manners. When a seven-year-old passes the time in his carpool screaming invented phrases involving foul words, this is not creativity. Or perhaps it is creativity, but creativity run amuck, degenerated into rudeness and coarseness.

One of the most important parental roles is to teach the concept of "self-regulation"—at core, the ability of children to control their behavior to comply with an acceptable standard of civility. As important as is creativity, it cannot be allowed to run roughshod over decorum. Creativity thrives on breaking breakable rules and altering everyday expectations, but this is no excuse for bad manners.

> Striving to improve a child's creativity is not, and cannot be, work.

Certainly rules can be broken in the pursuit of creativity. But just because something is a "rule" doesn't mean it must be broken. No child's creativity is harmed by being required to respect other people or by being encouraged to develop the self-regulation necessary to act accordingly.

One important piece of a young child's natural creativity is a lack of socially imposed inhibitions. The lack of inhibitions helps a young child to free associate, to investigate, to experiment, to try things without judgment.

This particular part of a child's creative instinct is what can cause the most parental distress. Lack of inhibition in small children often runs headlong into a parent's sense of propriety and structure. It is not unusual for parents to thwart small moments of creativity for the sake of etiquette or what passes for politeness.

Six Ways to Avoid Squashing Creativity

Don't Hover
Creativity often involves taking risks, which is the last thing a child is liable to do under surveillance. Step back and give your child some breathing room.

Don't Judge
Children should think in terms of how satisfied they are with their accomplishments, not how they will be evaluated or graded or what other people will think of their work.

Don't Reward
Excessively rewarding children with gold stars, money, or toys for their creative work tends to deprive a child of the innate joy of creating, which itself is the greatest reward of all.

Don't Compete
Avoid putting your child in stark win–lose situations when it comes to creative activities. Sure, competition is a way of life, but creativity is something different. Different forms of creativity cannot be compared as can the records of two football teams.

Don't Micro-Manage
Yes, it's your parental responsibility to instruct your child, but giving detailed instructions makes originality and exploration seem superfluous.

Don't Restrict Choices
Creativity is encouraged when children feel free to follow wherever their curiosity leads them, so allow your child to choose whatever interests her, and then support the interest.

Here is where you need that sense of balance. Is the rule of "etiquette" in question really an important one for a four-year-old? Will allowing the child to break this rule really mean teaching her to disrespect others? Or is this rule a formality that can be postponed to a more appropriate age?

In making that decision remember this: Small children rarely recall the "polite" lesson a parent may try to teach through such an experience. But the creativity lesson—the anti-creativity lesson, that is—may have a lasting impact. As parents we must be careful to nurture the creative spirit; as easily as creativity can be developed, just as surely it can be stifled.

> The more spontaneous you can be, the more creative your child will become.

As parents, we also tend to focus on imposing structure, which is surely necessary, both practically and emotionally in the chaotic world of children. But keep in mind that the reason for the structure is to help develop a sense of security and self-esteem, not to teach them that structure itself is more important than imagination or mystery.

There are plenty of times when children cannot be allowed to do things that are inappropriate or dangerous. And there are basic responsibilities they must be taught. But how many times do parents say no when their children ask, say, to play with the Play-Doh® simply because the parents, not unreasonably, don't have the time or energy to clean the little red and blue and yellow crumbs off the floor when playtime is over? And how many of our more guarded, inhibited sensibilities do we thoughtlessly pass along to our children *well before they need them*?

Toddlers need limits, but beware of making unnecessary rules. Limiting behavior too strictly to what is "right" may teach the lesson that every experiment or innovation is "wrong." Yes, it's wrong to pop your little sister's new balloon. But coloring the tree purple rather than green is just one more experiment in the history of art. Always allow some room for experimentation.

A Framework for Action

As we've already discussed, creativity is not just arts and crafts. Albert Einstein was creative, as were Henry Ford and Mahatma Ghandi. But these people, and countless like them, were creative in ways that have nothing to do with the arts. Underlying any creative effort is a fertile imagination—and the well-developed imagination leads a person toward the four basic creativity behaviors.

Part Two contains four chapters of creativity-enhancing activities. Chapter 5, the first chapter in Part Two, is called "Imagination Games." These activities encourage children to think "outside the box" by combining their thoughts in unexpected ways. These games can provide many hours of stretching the imagination, of creativity-building fun.

Although creativity is not just about art, there is no denying the connection between visual expressiveness and the creative spirit. Therefore, in Chapter 6, you'll find "Arts, Crafts, and Projects." Some of these activities involve traditional arts and crafts materials; others employ less conventional supplies. In all cases, the point is to make the connection between things your child can produce with his or her hands and the ideas they can dream up.

Child-development experts stress the importance of listening to—and telling—stories in developing the imagination. You'll find a wealth of activities that draw out and play upon this important piece of the creativity puzzle in Chapter 7, "Story-telling, Performance, and Fantasy."

Some aspects of creativity resist labeling and pigeonholing. Almost any sort of engaging interaction between parent and child and between child and the world can enhance creativity in a wondrous way. Thus Chapter 8 is entitled "Creative Experiences" and groups together an invigorating mix of things to do that defy strict categorization.

All four chapters in Part Two contain activities and games that will spark both on-the-spot fun and nurture long-term creativity. All activities are open-ended and flexible; descriptions should be taken as suggestions rather than rules.

Many of the activities require only your time and attention. When materials are necessary, they will be listed at the top of the page. You may wish to begin to accumulate the kinds of items that can kindle or enhance creativity; a starter list of materials is provided at the beginning of Chapter 6.

Browse through the offerings; pick and choose according to your interests, your children's interests, your current mood, or pure whim. Remember that creativity resents excessive structure. Whatever you do, do not turn "creativity time" into another slot in your child's busy schedule. The more spontaneous you can be, the more creative your child will become.

PART TWO

Activities and
Games

A **well-developed imagination** is at the center of a child's creativity. Without the ability to conceive new images, dream up
new approaches to the world, and think new thoughts, a child
will never fully experience the creativity that is his or her
birthright.

And so, at the heart of all of the activities and games that follow in this part of the book, there is an imaginative enterprise
of one sort or another. Although you will be shown just how to
"train" your children to develop the four behaviors that under-
lie adult creativity, remember not to approach the activities as
some sort of "training." Children who sense a purpose when
an adult is playing with them will not play with heart or spirit,
nor will they play for long.

Note to parents: The activities within each section are
grouped into four age ranges: preschoolers, kindergartners,
first and second graders, and third graders and older. Please
recognize that many of the activities are appropriate for a wide
range of ages:

☆ An activity marked with a "+" is also appropriate for an older age group.

At the bottom of each activity or game, you will see a checklist, consisting of the following items:

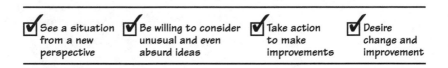

☑ See a situation from a new perspective	☑ Be willing to consider unusual and even absurd ideas	☑ Take action to make improvements	☑ Desire change and improvement

The checklist is a simple, easy way for you to know which one (or more) of the four creative behaviors an activity will bring out in your child.

CHAPTER FIVE

Imagination Games

"Imagination is more important than knowledge."
—ALBERT EINSTEIN

The games in this section are the easiest of all, requiring nothing but time and thought on the part of both parent and child. These games are great to play in the car, in the grocery store, in the kitchen while you're preparing a meal, or while your child is waiting for a special visitor to arrive. Because of the thoughtful nature of these activities, many of the games are more appropriate for older children. Remember to encourage "thinking time" and to prompt a hesitant child with gentle, open-ended questions rather than leading questions. Accept silliness, tolerate the off-beat, and most importantly, have fun.

* Curious Cuisine +

(paper and pencil optional)

While you're preparing a meal, when you're grocery shopping, or any other time the talk turns to food, launch your child on a culinary flight of fancy by asking him to invent new, unlikely sounding meals out of totally inappropriate ingredients.

He can start with the main course—fried peacock toes on a bed of chocolate-covered cotton balls, perhaps? Scrambled worms with onions and feathers? From there he can move on to soup, appetizer, or dessert.

If your child is school age, you might suggest that he create a whole menu's worth of dishes and give the restaurant an appropriately "awful" name.

You could also approach the game from a recipe point of view. Start by suggesting a fanciful name for a dish and have your child concoct the list of ingredients necessary to create it. Have him supply the necessary cooking instructions, too. To push his imagination further, have him think of some new place to cook it other than the oven. While having fun, your child will actually be learning how to think unconventionally.

Remember:
Activities marked with a "+" are good for older children, too!

| ☐ Desire change and improvement | ☐ See a situation from a new perspective | ☑ Be willing to consider unusual and even absurd ideas | ☐ Take action to make improvements |

* Design Your Own. . . +

This game is fun to play while you're waiting somewhere because you can lead your child into reimagining an otherwise ordinary and familiar place.

Let's say you're in the airport, waiting to board your plane. Your child is tired of coloring in the coloring book she brought along and is bored with looking out of the window at the various service trucks getting the plane ready. Here's what you can say to her: "Okay, you've been in the airport a while and you know what the airport looks like. What if you could design an airport yourself? What would yours have that regular airports don't have?"

> "What if you could design an airport yourself?"

The airport, of course, is just an example. You could ask about the car if you're stuck in traffic or even about your house if you're home together and there's "nothing to do." To keep the conversation developing, be sure to ask questions about your child's ideas. Ask her why she'd want a particular feature she describes. Ask her what materials she'd use to make it, how long it would take to build, and perhaps how she would describe it in a commercial.

Listen closely to her descriptions and offer questions in response. Your queries will urge her to question assumptions she may be making along the way.

| ☑ Desire change and improvement | ☑ See a situation from a new perspective | ☐ Be willing to consider unusual and even absurd ideas | ☐ Take action to make improvements |

* Animal Day +

If you think about it, it's kind of hard to figure out what animals actually do all day. Here's a game that urges your child to fill in the gaps of our knowledge with his imagination.

Ask your child to name an animal, and then have him describe a typical day in the life of that animal. Begin when the animal first wakes up. Perhaps the animal proceeds through a human-like day—this supposition alone would require your child to look at the world from an unexpected angle. If necessary, prompt your child with questions that help him combine his knowledge of his own routines with speculation about the animal. "What does the frog eat for breakfast?" you might ask. "Who does he play with? What are his favorite television shows and computer games?"

Different children will respond differently to this game. Some may try to be realistic; others may instantly create jobs and shopping experiences for bunnies and salamanders. Merely transferring a human day onto a salamander may not sound completely creative, but for young children, it's a first step toward improving three creative behaviors at once: thinking outside the box, questioning assumptions, and suspending belief.

If your child responds well, you can push him further by saying something like, "How do you know salamanders eat breakfast when they first get up? Maybe they eat dinner in the morning," or "Maybe they only eat breakfast on Mondays," or some other comment that pushes him to question the premise further.

| ☐ Desire change and improvement | ☑ See a situation from a new perspective | ☑ Be willing to consider unusual and even absurd ideas | ☐ Take action to make improvements |

* Couplets +

A couplet is a set of two lines that have roughly the same rhythm and end in a rhyme, such as "April showers/Bring May flowers." Here's a chance for your child to create her own couplets.

Start by "seeding" the couplet with a first line. If your last name can be rhymed, have your child try to make a couplet using her full name (such as "Tracy Susan Miller/Don't hide behind the pillar!"). Or look for random phrases around the house, perhaps on packages of food ("Free Recipe Under the Label") or on articles of clothing ("Gentle cycle, do not bleach"). Couplets are most fun when there is some effort to make a bit of sense, even if it's nonsensical sense. So if you can, steer your child away from completely random non sequiturs. This bit of structure is not intended to inhibit creativity so much as to encourage creativity with a purpose.

This activity works especially well when you can use bill-boards you pass for first lines. And time will seem to pass quicker when you and your child are having a silly old time.

| ☐ Desire change and improvement | ☐ See a situation from a new perspective | ☑ Be willing to consider unusual and even absurd ideas | ☑ Take action to make improvements |

* Make a List +

(what you need: pencil and paper)

Games that involve a combination of imagination and observation can be particularly effective in nurturing creativity in children. This one requires the parent to do some writing if the child isn't old enough to write; older children can manage this game almost entirely by themselves.

The premise is simple: have your child locate and list items in the house that can be grouped under an interesting heading that you name. For example, things that stretch. Things that can break. Things that are taller than he is. Things in piles. This exercise subtly prompts him to look at everyday objects with a new perspective.

Have a smaller child come up with only five or six items per list. Older children can be given a time limit of, say, fifteen minutes. Once he's played it a few times, an older child may also begin to devise some unusual—and creative—list categories of his own.

| ☐ Desire change and improvement | ☑ See a situation from a new perspective | ☐ Be willing to consider unusual and even absurd ideas | ☐ Take action to make improvements |

* Backwards World +

A longtime favorite "special" day at some schools and summer camps is Backwards Day, when children are encouraged to wear whatever they can backwards. An imaginative counterpart to that activity is Backwards World.

Ask your child to imagine a world in which *everything* is done backwards from the way we do it now. Then have her pick a particular location or a particular activity and imagine how it works in Backwards World.

There's wonderful room for variation in this game. For instance, one child may say that in Backwards World, you pay for your groceries before you buy them. Another child might interpret things a little differently and say that in Backwards World, the grocery store pays you to shop there.

Of course everyone drives in reverse in Backwards World, but ask your child to imagine what other changes this might entail. Do cars have their headlights in the back? Do people get speeding tickets for going too slowly?

One thing's for sure: you must suspend all logic and judgment when entering Backwards World.

| ☐ Desire change and improvement | ☑ See a situation from a new perspective | ☑ Be willing to consider unusual and even absurd ideas | ☐ Take action to make improvements |

IMAGINATION GAMES FOR KINDERGARTNERS

* If Buildings Could Talk +

This game works very well in the car during local trips—around town running errands or to and from school. As you move along a busy street, pick out a building you're passing slowly or have stopped in front of and have your child create a life for it. What kind of personality does the building have? Is it kind or scatterbrained or loyal or stern? What is its name? The

> The more surprising the question, the better.

idea here is to stretch those imaginative muscles as far as they will go. Ask your child what the building's job is. Who are its brothers and sisters and cousins? What does it like to do for fun? What does its voice sound like? What are its favorite foods?

Your efforts here are directed at opening your child's mind in unexpected ways. The more surprising the question, the better. Respond to your child's answers with probing follow-up questions. If he sees a large building and says that the building would have a deep, gruff voice, ask him why its voice couldn't be high and squeaky. Without dampening his fun, see where you can push a bit to have him question his original statement and expand his thinking.

| ☐ Desire change and improvement | ☑ See a situation from a new perspective | ☑ Be willing to consider unusual and even absurd ideas | ☐ Take action to make improvements |

* Similes +

In a simpler time, this was a parlor game: one person said the first part of a well-known simile, and someone else had to complete it. "Sly as a..." "Fox!" "Busy as a..." "Beaver!"

In this game your child can invent some of her own, brand-new similes. These should make sense rather than be silly, but they should be her own creation. You can start her off with some ideas, like:

☆ clean as a...
☆ awesome as a...
☆ quiet as a...
☆ tired as a...

The only requirement here is that the simile be utterly new. After your child gets the hang of it, her inventive spirit will take over and she'll be able to create a few without any help from you.

| ☐ Desire change and improvement | ☐ See a situation from a new perspective | ☑ Be willing to consider unusual and even absurd ideas | ☑ Take action to make improvements |

* Alien Invasion +

Part of a young child's creative spirit arises from the fresh perspective he instinctively brings to the world. This game actively taps into that perspective and is especially fun to play with children who might be getting a little too used to the way things look, behave, and operate.

The premise is borrowed from any number of hackneyed science fiction plots in which beings from another planet come to Earth and either don't understand or misinterpret common sights or actions. In this case, you and your child pretend to be aliens fresh off the spaceship. Look around. What do you see? How do you explain it?

This game works best when you are driving around town or are out taking a walk. If you see someone walking a dog, ask your child who is walking whom. If you see a row of parking meters, you might comment, "Look at the skinny robots! Why aren't they moving?" If you're in the house, you might want to begin with a look out a window. If you see a tree, you can ask your alien child what sort of creature he thinks that is. What does it do with all those little green things? Your child will have fun while he learns to look at everyday objects from a brand new perspective.

Yes, this is one of those games that requires a bit of creativity on your part as well. If you're at a loss and you need some hints about how to improvise creativity, look back to Chapter 4, where we use the example of a visit to an art museum to offer tips about "on the fly" creativity.

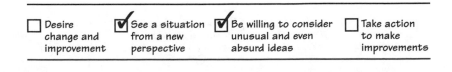

| ☐ Desire change and improvement | ☑ See a situation from a new perspective | ☑ Be willing to consider unusual and even absurd ideas | ☐ Take action to make improvements |

An offshoot of this game involves imagining yourselves to be on an alien planet. First you can "design" it: is it hot or cold? Are the oceans made of water, liquid, air, or maybe grape jelly? Do you feel really heavy or really light when you walk around? Then you can "explore." What do the beings there look like? What do they do all day? Why?

The best thing about an imaginary planet is that you can visit anytime you like, just by thinking creatively.

MORE IMAGINATION GAMES FOR KINDERGARTNERS

(see Preschooler section)
- ✕ Curious Cuisine
- ✕ Design Your Own...
- ✕ Animal Day
- ✕ Couplets
- ✕ Make a List
- ✕ Backwards World

* Mnifty Mnemonics

How can we ever forget Roy G. Biv? That's the point: we can't. It's probably the most well-known mnemonic we learned as children, invented to remind us of the colors of the rainbow: red, orange, yellow, green, blue, indigo, violet. Many of us also remember the sentence, "My very educated mother just served us nine pickles," which was used to teach the order of planets in the solar system—until a couple of years ago, at least, when Neptune moved to a more distant point from the sun than Pluto. Now our very educated mother has to serve us peanut noodles or pine nuts.

Mnemonics are fun to create, and creating them provides an engaging exercise that subtly reinforces the idea that the world can always be approached from an unexpected vantage point and that problems can be solved in the process. For this exercise, have your child think of a series of related words she'd like to remember—the names of your neighbors, the last ten World Series champions, her seven favorite ice cream flavors, almost anything at all—and then use the initial letters from each word to create a memorable sentence.

Creating mnemonics is not just a fun game, it's a skill your child can use throughout her life to remember hard-to-recall facts.

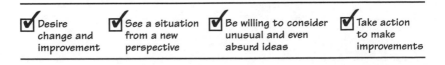

☑ Desire change and improvement   ☑ See a situation from a new perspective   ☑ Be willing to consider unusual and even absurd ideas   ☑ Take action to make improvements

* What Do You See?

(paper and pencil optional)

While imagination is free-form and works best in an uninhibited mode, it is underscored by a highly concrete skill: observation. For instance, the writer most capable of close observation can convert his imagination into a compelling narrative—which, in turn, can light up the imaginations of all who read his work.

Have your child go into a room in your home and look intently at one corner or one section of the room for about thirty seconds. Then have him come back and tell you, or write down, everything he saw there. Encourage as much detail as possible: numbers of objects, kinds of items, colors and shapes, precise location, even texture. When he's thought of everything he can, go back in the room together and see how much he actually recalled.

Then try it again in another corner of the room or in a different room altogether. This is a game that will substantively improve your child's observational skills if played often enough.

An alternate version of the game involves clothing. With a dress-up bin full of accessories like hats, gloves, scarves, shoes, belts, vests, and so on, assemble an outlandish outfit for yourself. When you're ready, call your child in to look at you for ten seconds, after which he must leave the room and either tell you or write down exactly what you were wearing. And just for fun, give your child a turn at dressing up and see how well you do in the observational mode. You may need more practice than you think!

| ☐ Desire change and improvement | ☑ See a situation from a new perspective | ☐ Be willing to consider unusual and even absurd ideas | ☐ Take action to make improvements |

* Connections +

Name two unrelated items. Now have your child think of a connection between the two. It's as simple—and as complicated—as that.

> Have your child think of a connection between two unrelated items.

You might say, "Telescope and porcupine." What might your child say? Who knows? It might be something reasonably concrete: "Telescopes are mostly black and white and so are porcupines." Or it might be something completely whimsical: "Because the zookeeper felt the porcupines were too dangerous to be near, she put them in a special house so far away you need a telescope to see them."

And in case you were wondering, you get a chance to play the game, too. Think it's easy to continue to connect two unrelated words? Try it and find out! You and your child will be surprised at how far your mental muscles will stretch.

| ☐ Desire change and improvement | ☑ See a situation from a new perspective | ☑ Be willing to consider unusual and even absurd ideas | ☐ Take action to make improvements |

* Letter Sentences +

From a young age, children are exposed to picture books of the alphabet. Creating Letter Sentences gives them the opportunity to create—aurally—a sort of alphabet book of their own. Letter Sentences is another imaginative game that focuses your child's thinking within a particular structure; the idea is to encourage unexpected associations within a problem-solving context.

Beginning with the letter A, have your child concoct a simple sentence in which all the words begin with that letter. You might offer an example, such as "Alice ate apples." But, depending on your child's temperament and tastes, feel free to be far sillier than that. "Arthur adores artificial air" might work. Or perhaps "All astronauts are allergic."

On to letter B. If your child catches on quickly, have her make her sentence first, and then you can follow. If she needs a bit more modeling, you can continue going first for a few letters. With older children, you can make all words begin with the chosen letters. Younger children may like the opportunity to use the words "the" or "a" or "of" when they want to.

Few children have the stamina to finish the entire alphabet in one session. Try to remember where you left off so you can start there the next time. You and your child will have to be especially creative when you reach the letter X, but with all the practice you'll have had with the first twenty-three letters of the alphabet, you're sure to find a solution.

| ☐ Desire change and improvement | ☐ See a situation from a new perspective | ☑ Be willing to consider unusual and even absurd ideas | ☑ Take action to make improvements |

MORE IMAGINATION GAMES FOR
1ST AND 2ND GRADERS

(see Preschooler section)

✹ Curious Cuisine

✹ Design Your Own...

✹ Animal Day

✹ Couplets

✹ Make a List

✹ Backwards World

(see Kindergartner section)

✹ If Buildings Could Talk

✹ Similes

✹ Alien Invasion

* Renaming the Planets

The names we use for the planets in our solar system date back to the ancient Romans; the names chosen related the appearance of the five planets that were known at that point—Mercury, Venus, Mars, Jupiter, and Saturn—to the behavior of the gods for whom they were named. The planets that have been discovered since then have also been named for ancient gods.

Give your child a chance to rename the planets according to some other scheme. What would he name the planets if he could change their names? And why? Or extend the idea of questioning the premise even further by suggesting to him that those moving objects he sees in the sky at night may not be planets at all. What else could they be? Why? By questioning "common knowledge," your child has a chance to exercise his imagination.

| ☑ Desire change and improvement | ☑ See a situation from a new perspective | ☑ Be willing to consider unusual and even absurd ideas | ☑ Take action to make improvements |

* New School

Once your child has been in school a couple of years, she has a pretty good sense of how the school day proceeds and what sorts of activities she can expect to do there. Here's a chance to let her imagination run around a bit within her familiar routine.

Begin by asking her what subject she might like to study at school if she could choose anything at all—something her real school doesn't teach. Then have her pretend that she's in charge of a school that's completely different from any school anywhere in the world. What would the school day there be like? What subjects would the children learn? Have her write up the schedule of a typical day at this highly atypical school. Or even have her act it out.

By doing this exercise, you may discover that your child likes a particular subject that you never knew she had an interest in. Just as important, your child will have a chance to see a familiar place from a new perspective.

| ☑ Desire change and improvement | ☑ See a situation from a new perspective | ☑ Be willing to consider unusual and even absurd ideas | ☐ Take action to make improvements |

* Recipes

(what you need: paper and pencil)

Many children know that recipes are used to make favorite dishes in the kitchen. This imagination-stretcher takes the idea of a recipe and applies it in unexpected places.

Begin by having your child explain what a recipe is. This will help him put the concept into words, which may prove useful when you then ask him to write down a recipe for friendship. Or a recipe for excitement. Or a recipe for trouble! In doing so, he'll be using a familiar concept in a totally new way.

If your child likes this activity, you can have him gather his recipes and make a very special kind of "cookbook" out of them. You may wish to make copies of this special collection to share with other family members. It's sure to be a treasured keepsake.

| ☐ Desire change and improvement | ☑ See a situation from a new perspective | ☐ Be willing to consider unusual and even absurd ideas | ☑ Take action to make improvements |

MORE IMAGINATION GAMES FOR
3RD GRADERS AND OLDER

(see Preschooler section)
- ☆ Design Your Own...
- ☆ Couplets

(see Kindergartner section)
- ☆ If Buildings Could Talk
- ☆ Similes

(see 1st and 2nd Grader section)
- ☆ Mnifty Mnemonics
- ☆ Connections
- ☆ Letter Sentences

CHAPTER SIX

Arts, Crafts, and Projects

"To have a great idea, have a lot of them."
—THOMAS EDISON

We warned you earlier that sometimes you just have to get messy when you're being creative. But don't worry—not every activity in this chapter will leave your child (and you) covered in paint or glue or paper scraps.

Each activity in this section comes with a list of suggested materials, but feel free to substitute. Use your imagination!

If you want to feel as if your household is generally prepared for spontaneous creativity, here's a master list of all the items used in the activities in this section, plus a few more suggestions thrown in for good measure.

Stuff for making other stuff:
* paper towel and toilet
  paper tubes
* old bedsheets
* boxes, all sizes
* paper bags
* egg cartons

* scrap paper
* old magazines
* junk mail
* tape
* string
* old shoelaces

- ☆ plastic straws
- ☆ assorted kitchen items
- ☆ scissors
- ☆ glue stick
- ☆ parcel paper
- ☆ old newspapers
- ☆ stapler
- ☆ clay
- ☆ mail order catalogs
- ☆ buttons
- ☆ cardboard, all sizes
- ☆ construction paper
- ☆ rubber bands
- ☆ paper clips
- ☆ old socks
- ☆ empty spools (especially wooden)
- ☆ toothpicks
- ☆ plain white paper
- ☆ white paper plates
- ☆ poster board
- ☆ "reject" photographs
- ☆ used gift wrap
- ☆ "interesting pictures" file (see the game called "Categories")
- ☆ index cards
- ☆ wooden clothespins

Stuff for drawing:

- ☆ crayons
- ☆ pens
- ☆ cotton swabs
- ☆ old toothbrushes
- ☆ sponges
- ☆ washable markers
- ☆ watercolor paints
- ☆ colored pencils
- ☆ chalk

ARTS, CRAFTS, AND PROJECTS FOR PRESCHOOLERS

* Partial Pictures +

(what you need: paper; crayons or markers)

On a blank sheet of paper, take a crayon and make a suggestive but abstract shape or line. Hand the paper to your child and tell him to make a picture using your squiggle as a starting point. Encourage him to turn the paper in any direction he wants.

If he needs prodding, you might suggest a general type of picture—perhaps an animal, spaceship, or building. Allow him to take his time and use his imagination. Try not to complete anything for him, and keep your suggestions open and nonjudgmental. For instance, if he's drawing an animal, don't say, "Shouldn't you put a tail here?"; instead, you might ask, "Is there anything else that you think this animal should have?" Encourage unusual perspectives and unexpected additions.

> Encourage unusual perspectives.

When the picture is done, have your child create a story around what he's drawn. That way, he'll not only create art with his hands, he'll also get a chance to use his imagination. Remember that no special artistic ability is required, and the final drawings do not have to "look like" anything to be recognized and "interpreted" by your child.

Remember:
Activities marked with a "+" are good for older children, too!

| ☑ Desire change and improvement | ☑ See a situation from a new perspective | ☑ Be willing to consider unusual and even absurd ideas | ☑ Take action to make improvements |

* Wacky Necklaces +

(what you need: heavy string or old shoelaces, assortment of dry pasta, Cheerios® or Froot Loops®, plastic straws, other small items that can be strung)

There's nothing wrong with stringing beads, of course. But how about making this project more creative? Anything lightweight, reasonably small, and with a hole somewhere near the middle is fair game to be strung by a wacky necklace maker.

Here's an activity that your child can do more or less on her own after you've done a bit of gathering. Pasta is always a good bet for starters. (For a truly stunning necklace, you might sit with your child and have her color the pasta with markers before stringing it.) Plastic straws cut into one-inch or so lengths make for nice patterns. Cheerios® or Froot Loops® work well. The possibilities are limited only by your imaginations. Small nuts or washers from the basement workshop might be nice. Small spools from the sewing box. Lifesavers®. Tires that have fallen off toy cars. If you've got a hole-puncher and some old playing cards, cut them up and use them too. Be sure to ask your child for suggestions as well, and use this discussion to prompt her along the lines of the four basic creative behaviors.

And, oh yes, you might want to throw in an actual bead or two while you're at it.

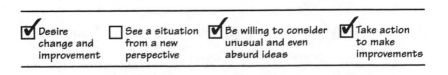

| ☑ Desire change and improvement | ☐ See a situation from a new perspective | ☑ Be willing to consider unusual and even absurd ideas | ☑ Take action to make improvements |

* Sorting Table +

(what you need: large piece of cardboard or poster board [at least 18 by 24 inches]; black marker; two or three boxes of assorted objects of varying shapes, colors, and, textures [buttons, blocks, spools, etc.])

On the cardboard or poster board, draw two circles or ovals next to each other, surrounded by a larger rectangle, like this:

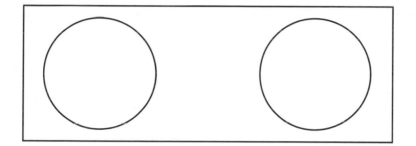

Put the board on a table along with two or three boxes of objects mixed together. For younger children, you may want to start with merely two types of things to sort—say, buttons and blocks. Have your child sort the objects by type, putting the buttons in one circle and the blocks in the other.

After this structured introduction to sorting, encourage your child to sort the objects another way, and see if he can explain his effort to you.

For older children, present a larger variety of objects and have them sort by shape or size or color or material—the wooden objects in the left circle, perhaps, and the plastic ones in the right. You can combine characteristics also, asking your

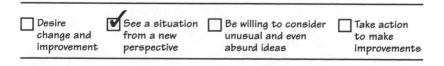

☐ Desire change and improvement ☑ See a situation from a new perspective ☐ Be willing to consider unusual and even absurd ideas ☐ Take action to make improvements

child to put the red round ones in one circle, and the blue square ones in the other.

Once the suggested sorting has been done, have your child sort the objects in a different way of his own devising. This exercise will encourage him to see the objects from a different perspective. When he's done, see if you can guess how he's sorted them.

* Coloring Box +

(what you need: extra-large corrugated cardboard box, flat white latex paint, black permanent marker, washable markers)

This activity involves a bit of set-up, so if you're looking for something fast and easy, skip it for now. On the other hand, this is a very special treat of an activity; it even works nicely at a birthday party.

First, find a very large box, such as the kind a refrigerator or oven comes in. This may not be that easy. Try calling local appliance stores; you should eventually find someone who can set one aside for you. Transporting it to your house may not be easy either, depending on the size of your car.

Once the box is at your house, set it up on newspaper in the garage or outside and paint the whole thing white with flat latex paint. (You don't have to paint the side that will sit on the ground.) Let it dry. Then, take a black permanent marker and draw a scene that your child, or a number of children, can color in. You might make the whole box look like a house, with windows, a door, a picket fence around it, flowers, and so forth. Or you could make it look like the main street of a small town. Or a fire station. Or anything you'd like.

What you're creating, in effect, is something of a three-dimensional coloring book. Make your design so that there are both large and small areas to color in. And leave plenty of plain white space for free-form drawing as well. If your box looks

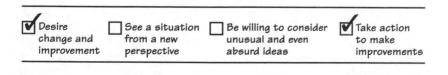

☑ Desire change and improvement   ☐ See a situation from a new perspective   ☐ Be willing to consider unusual and even absurd ideas   ☑ Take action to make improvements

like a building, you might cut the box to create actual doors or windows.

Make sure the washable markers are relatively new, then hand them over to the children and watch them go to work. Don't worry about how well they stay in the lines—the purpose is to push the child's imagination, not to set limits on artistic vision.

* Scrambimals +

(what you need: age-appropriate drawing materials)

Ask your child to name two of her favorite animals. Now ask her to imagine that these two animals could magically become a single creature. Prompt her to give the new animal a new name. Then have her draw the fabulous beast.

Next, have her create a story explaining how this new animal came to exist and what its life is like. Where does it live? What does it eat? What does it like doing best? Why? What other animals are its friends? Why? Urge her to add some of these elements to the drawing.

When this imaginary animal seems fully fleshed out, try a new creation with a new combination of animals. Or have your

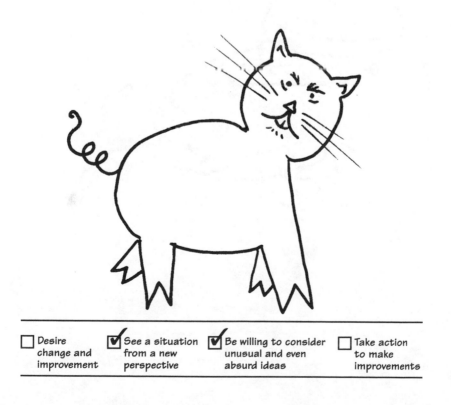

| ☐ Desire change and improvement | ☑ See a situation from a new perspective | ☑ Be willing to consider unusual and even absurd ideas | ☐ Take action to make improvements |

child flex her creativity even further by making up a whole new creature—one that neither she nor anyone else has ever seen or heard of before. Depending on your child's attention span and enthusiasm for this game, you might have her create a zoo full of animals, then staple together the drawings in a book with a construction paper cover.

This game will help your child to associate two unique ideas (two different animals, in this case) and draw conclusions that she might never have considered on her own.

* Crazycakes (an edible project!) +

(what you need: pancake batter of your choice, large frying pan or griddle)

Anyone can make round pancakes. How about pouring that batter onto the griddle with a little less inhibition! The aim here is a sort of Rorschach pancake—abstract shapes that conjure images and stories in a hungry gang of breakfast eaters. It's kind of like cloud-watching on your plate. The only rule to this game is that no pancake can be eaten until someone's imagination turns it into something else.

Here's a variation for those who prefer round pancakes. Dribble a thin line of batter onto the griddle to draw a design, then, as the edges of the design firm up, cover the entire thing with more batter to create a standard, round pancake. Once you flip it, you'll see your original "drawing" on top. This can also be "interpreted" just as the free-form pancakes above.

One final twist here is to allow older children to make their own designs or drawings. Use extreme caution, of course, since the pancake pan is very hot. Once the crazycakes are served, you won't have to ask your children twice to "clean up" *this* project.

| ☐ Desire change and improvement | ☑ See a situation from a new perspective | ☑ Be willing to consider unusual and even absurd ideas | ☐ Take action to make improvements |

* Color Cubes

(what you need: empty plastic ice-cube tray, food coloring, small plastic eye-dropper, paper towels)

Young children are fascinated by the effects of mixing colors, and this is one of the easiest, least messy, and most satisfying ways of offering them free rein in their experimentation.

> No rules or guide-lines here, just the pure pleasure of satisfying curiosity.

Begin with a plastic ice-cube tray in which each cube holder is half-filled with water. Take three or so drops of blue food coloring and turn one of the compartments blue. Likewise create a red compartment and a yellow one so you now have three (primary) colored "cubes" of water. Add a bit more water to these cubes to make them more full than the others.

Set the tray down on a couple of layers of paper toweling at a good work table for your child. Give him a plastic eye-dropper (the kind that comes with infants' acetaminophen works well for this) and demonstrate how, for instance, you can mix a drop of blue water with a few drops of yellow water to turn the water in one of the plain cubes green.

After that, stand back and let your child experiment. He may come up with some lovely shades of lavender or aqua, or he may be one who likes to turn everything brown. There are no rules and no guidelines here, just the pure pleasure of satisfying curiosity. Encourage your child to continue to experiment in changing tones and shades even after all the clear water is gone.

☑ Desire   ☐ See a situation   ☐ Be willing to consider   ☑ Take action
change and   from a new   unusual and even   to make
improvement   perspective   absurd ideas   improvements

While this concrete experiment in color mixing is going on, you might talk to your child about other things that mix together and fantasize together about what it might be like if things that normally don't mix—say, buildings and crocodiles—could.

* Brushless Painting +

(what you need: large sheets of paper, washable paints, 8-inch lengths of string, cotton swabs, old toothbrushes, sponges, scissors)

Can't find a paintbrush when your child feels like painting? No problem at all. Time for some brushless painting!

Provide your child a good work surface and plenty of clothing protection. This activity works better on a table than an easel. To begin, have her dip about half the length of a string into one of the paints, let it drip a bit, then drag it along the paper to create designs. When it runs out of paint, she can either redip it or take a new string and dip it into another color and add to her painting.

Another good way to paint without brushes is with a cotton swab, which can be held as either a paint brush or a pencil. Old toothbrushes can provide a unique painting experience also. Encourage your child to use her imagination about what she thinks might be usable in place of a paint brush. Don't dismiss any idea outright; if her idea is inappropriate or unworkable, explain why, make related suggestions, continue to brainstorm together. Raw wagon wheel pasta? Could work! A plastic fork? Why not!

One last option to consider is the sponge method. You can start with simple two-inch squares, or you can use scissors to create all kinds of shapes. Before your child begins sponge painting, wet the sponge and then squeeze out all the water. Let your child experiment with different application methods. And remember not to worry about a little bit of mess. This is painting, after all. And she's not even using a brush.

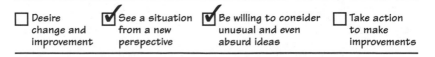

| ☐ Desire change and improvement | ☑ See a situation from a new perspective | ☑ Be willing to consider unusual and even absurd ideas | ☐ Take action to make improvements |

* Categories

(what you need: an "interesting pictures" file)

You've been cutting out and saving items in an "interesting pictures" file, haven't you? Comprised of fun stuff found in magazines and catalogs? Stored in a neatly labeled ten- by thirteen-inch envelope?

Well, okay, you probably haven't. But it's a great idea, and it's not difficult to do. Once you have this file, it's handy for simple collages or for activities such as this one.

The idea here is simple: have your child go through the pictures in search of everything that falls into a certain category. You can have him put all the pictures of people into one pile, or all the pictures of food. Younger children should be allowed to concentrate on one category at a time, but older children might be given three or four categories at once.

When all the pictures in a given category are sorted, have your child sort within that category. If the subject is food, have him divide it into things you eat for dessert and things you don't eat for dessert. If it's a pile of vehicle pictures, separate the cars from the bicycles from the planes and so forth. Once the pictures are sorted, you can help your child question the premise of sorting by taking pictures from two different categories and asking him to invent a new category that could somehow encompass both of them.

| ☐ Desire change and improvement | ☑ See a situation from a new perspective | ☐ Be willing to consider unusual and even absurd ideas | ☐ Take action to make improvements |

For a greater challenge with an older child, have him create a new category that can incorporate pictures from three different "traditional" categories, or even four.

If this activity is one you think your child will enjoy, why not start your "interesting pictures" file today?

* What's Missing

(what you need: paper; crayon, marker, or pencil)

When young children are given the opportunity to observe carefully and then apply creative reasoning to their observations, their creativity is enhanced much the way artistic ability is enhanced by training in draftsmanship.

For this simple activity, sit down at a table with a piece of paper and a crayon, marker, or pencil. Tell your child you are going to draw a picture but leave some part of it out; she is to try to name what's missing. You might draw a house without a door, a face without a nose, a car without tires, or for a some-

| ☐ Desire change and improvement | ☑ See a situation from a new perspective | ☑ Be willing to consider unusual and even absurd ideas | ☐ Take action to make improvements |

what older child who has begun letter recognition, a stop sign without the letter O.

When your child has caught on and seems ready for an extra challenge, slide a blank page toward her and see what she can think to draw, and you can fill in the blank. Remember to encourage expression without worrying about accurate representation. If you're not sure what she's drawn, find out in a gentle way and then guess what's been left out.

A final twist to this activity comes when everyone's ready to be goofy. Then it's time to play What's Missing (Silly Version), in which the drawings are wacky and the missing items defy logic and reality. Draw an underwater castle with its rhinoceros missing or an airplane without its mailbox. Then hand a paper to your child and see where her imagination takes her, and you. And don't forget to giggle!

* Magazine Scavenger Hunt +

(what you need: old magazines, scissors, paper, glue stick)

There's nothing wrong with the old reliable collage for an entertaining, artistic activity. Here's a slight variation on it that keeps your child's mind a bit more active and adds an important bit of focus to a creative enterprise.

Bring out a stack of old magazines and tell your child he is about to go on a scavenger hunt without leaving his chair. (Younger children, of course, may need to be told what a scavenger hunt is.) For older children, you may want to prepare by writing out a list of pictures that might likely be found in a magazine—a car tire, a watch, a box of cereal, and so forth. (You can make the list appropriate for the sorts of magazines you have.) Have your child carefully cut the pictures out as he finds them.

For a younger child, rather than a longer list of diverse items, you might call out three categories of pictures and have him find as many things in those categories as he can: animals, food, and cars, if you want to keep it simple; or try "things you might find in your house" or "things you might find outside." Your child can look through the magazines on his own, but he will need your supervision when cutting out the pictures.

Once the items on the list are found or the magazines are exhausted, whichever comes first, have your child collect the

| ☐ Desire change and improvement | ☑ See a situation from a new perspective | ☑ Be willing to consider unusual and even absurd ideas | ☐ Take action to make improvements |

pictures together. If your child is older, tell him you want him to arrange the pictures in any order as long as any two pictures that are next to each other have something in common. When he is done, see if you can figure out the connections. A younger child can make a regular collage, or you can sit with him and make up a story from a handful of the collected pictures.

ARTS, CRAFTS, AND PROJECTS FOR KINDERGARTNERS

* Bad Photographs +

(what you need: construction paper, cardboard, glue stick, scissors, pens)

Everyone has photos that come back from the developer and are never shown again—the blurred portraits, the badly framed action shots, the picture of four kids in which at least one of them has her eyes closed, and so forth. But the funny thing is few of us have the discipline to throw them out. Here, finally, is something you can do with them.

First, find at least ten or twelve bad photographs. Now, very simply, let your child have fun with them. Let her cut them up and make a collage, or glue them onto cardboard to make little stand-up dolls, or glue little white "talking balloons" onto the pictures and have her think of funny things the people in the photos might be saying. If what she does turns out especially well, make some photocopies and send them to the friends and family members who appear in the photos; they're sure to enjoy your child's creation.

| ☑ Desire change and improvement | ☑ See a situation from a new perspective | ☑ Be willing to consider unusual and even absurd ideas | ☑ Take action to make improvements |

* Self-Portrait Dummy

(what you need: roll of brown parcel paper, scissors, crayons, markers, stapler, old newspaper)

A self-portrait is a time-honored method of self-expression. While this activity isn't as rule-bending as others, there is great value to encouraging expression based on your child's self-image. The end result is a life-sized self-portrait that might even turn into an imaginary playmate.

Start by unrolling a length of brown parcel paper on the floor. Have your child lie on it while you trace his outline in a dark, washable marker (being careful not to draw on his hair or his clothes). Repeat the process so you have two life-sized outlines. Next, leaving about a half-inch outside the line, cut the shapes out, or if your child is old enough, have him do the cutting.

Lay one of the shapes on a section of uncarpeted floor. Have your child turn the plain shape into a self-portrait, from head to toe. Encourage as much detail as he can think of, including patterns on clothing, shoe laces, and so forth. But do not limit your child to realistic details. Rather, encourage the self-portrait to be an image of himself as he appears in his dreams, or as he thinks other people see him, or any other way that will have him questioning some of his original premises about what a self-portrait might look like.

When he's done with that, he's only halfway through. Tell him that the other blank shape is going to be his back. Have

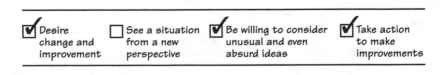

| ☑ Desire change and improvement | ☐ See a situation from a new perspective | ☑ Be willing to consider unusual and even absurd ideas | ☑ Take action to make improvements |

him draw and decorate it accordingly. You can use mirrors to show him what his back looks like. Again, you are encouraging fancy rather than slavish copying.

When both shapes are decorated, place them together so the self-portrait's front shows on one side and the back on the other. Staple them together, putting staples every few inches around the perimeter, but leave an eighteen-inch or so length unstapled. Crumple up sheets of old newspaper and use them to stuff the "body." When it's filled, staple the last eighteen inches closed. The self-portrait dummy is complete.

Or is it? Your child might want to put a hat on it, or a whistle on a string around its neck, or some other accessory. He might want to sit it down at his desk or lie it down in his bed. Now that the craft project is done, the imaginative play begins. Take cues from your child and follow where his imagination leads. It might be very interesting indeed to see how he plays with "himself" as another person.

* Progressive Art +

(what you need: paper, crayons or markers)

This is an older child's version of Partial Pictures. As with that activity, you begin by drawing one suggestive line on a sheet of paper. But rather than have your child draw an entire picture around your squiggle, have her add merely one or two more lines and then hand the picture back to you. You add a few more, then it's her turn again, and so on.

Progressive Art has a wonderful rhythm to it. At the beginning, neither of you may have a particular idea of what it is you're drawing. But at a certain point, a more cohesive design may make itself apparent, and you begin working toward that. And yet, a little later, it may look like something else entirely. Or the whole drawing may be one wonderfully expressive but abstract design. In any case, this activity will encourage experimentation and invention.

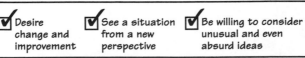

☑ Desire   ☑ See a situation   ☑ Be willing to consider   ☑ Take action
change and   from a new   unusual and even   to make
improvement   perspective   absurd ideas   improvements

* Alphabet Poster +

(what you need: old magazines and catalogs, poster board, scissors, glue stick)

One more variation on the collage theme is the Alphabet Poster. This time, your child searches through magazines and catalogs for one item for each letter of the alphabet.

Begin by dividing the poster board, with a light pencil line, into twenty-six boxes in whatever design you want. Lightly write in the alphabet, one letter per box. Then, open the magazines and go to work. The goal is to fill each box with an appropriate picture. Some children may like to proceed in alphabetical order, but it's not necessary. In fact, question the premise of those inclined to do so. What's so great about alphabetical order, you might ask? How about an alphabet poster on which the letters are listed in order of preference? Or some other order entirely?

Have your child glue the picture in the box in which he wants it, and if the child is old enough, have him write the letter in the corner of the box.

Certain letters present an obvious challenge—particularly X. If you get stuck, you can choose a picture of something that merely contains the letter that you're having trouble with. Or perhaps you and your child can brainstorm and think of your own creative way to approach such a challenge.

| ☐ Desire change and improvement | ☑ See a situation from a new perspective | ☑ Be willing to consider unusual and even absurd ideas | ☐ Take action to make improvements |

* Fold-a-Creature

(what you need: blank paper, pencils)

This is an activity that works especially well with three or more people, but two—you and your child—are fine. The description here assumes there are three people, with you as one of the participants. The easiest way to explain this game to a child will be by showing it in action.

Give each person a blank sheet of paper. You each begin by drawing, near the top, the head of some fantastic, imaginative creature or monster. The heads should be sized so that bodies can ultimately be drawn below them, and each head should end in a neck that is distinctly drawn beneath it, extending at least a half inch.

When everyone is done drawing the heads, they fold the paper down from the top so that only the two lines of the neck are visible. Then, pass your paper to the person on your left.

You will now have before you the creature begun by the person on your right, but all you can see is the bottom of the neck. Now it's your job to extend the drawing from the neck and create the middle section of the body: the shoulders, arms, torso, and hips. Draw absolutely any kind of body you can think of, without any knowledge of or concern for what sort of head lies under the folded section of paper. Again, be sure to size it so there will be room to draw legs. The bottom part of this section should end with the very tops of the legs. Once again, fold

---

☐ Desire change and improvement   ☐ See a situation from a new perspective   ☑ Be willing to consider unusual and even absurd ideas   ☑ Take action to make improvements

the paper down to this point, so that only the tops of the leg outlines are visible. And once again pass your paper to the person on your left.

Before you now is a creature begun by the other two people, awaiting its legs and feet. Outdo yourself with a flight of fancy here. When you're done, fold the paper one last time so that nothing drawn is visible, and pass the paper once more to the left.

In this example, the papers are now back to the person who started each creature. Time for unfolding, and unveiling the extraordinary beings that were drawn. You'll see that although each person was working from his or her own perspective, together you can create funny, scary, and altogether fantastic creatures. Be sure to have plenty of paper handy—most kids will want to do this activity over and over again.

MORE ARTS, CRAFTS, AND PROJECTS FOR KINDERGARTNERS

(see Preschooler section)

- Partial Pictures
- Wacky Necklaces
- Sorting Table
- Coloring Box
- Scrambimals
- Crazycakes
- Brushless Painting
- Magazine Scavenger Hunt

* Color Me Different

(what you need: paper; crayons or markers, including black)

Just at the age when a realistic streak often occurs in children, this exercise will keep some imaginative pathways open to more fanciful artistry.

Begin by having your child draw a scene using a black crayon or marker, drawing outlines only. When she's done, hand her all the colors and ask her to color in the scene—but she is not to make anything its natural color. If there's sky, it can't be blue or white or gray—let her make it purple or green. A house might be hot pink and red, a tree lavender and orange, a cat magenta or aquamarine.

This is not as odd as it might seem. Professional artists often sketch the world using unnatural colors. It helps shake up their compositional routines and can spark new flights of creativity.

| ☐ Desire change and improvement | ☐ See a situation from a new perspective | ☑ Be willing to consider unusual and even absurd ideas | ☑ Take action to make improvements |

* Toothpick Architecture

(what you need: box of round toothpicks; clay; paper, tape, markers [optional])

Here's a construction "toy" that your child can make himself. The premise is simple; the possibilities are endless.

Tell your child to roll the clay into a couple of dozen small balls, about a quarter- to a half-inch in diameter. These balls will be the corner joints that hold the toothpicks together. To demonstrate the basic concept, you might show your child how to make a square, add a sloping "A" frame, and repeat the process to make a three-dimensional house. He can leave the structure in its skeletal form, or he can tape paper to the frame and color the end result.

Another good structure to build is a small bridge. If you then attach the frame to a sheet of cardboard, your child can use it with small cars. With practice, his imagination will take over: there will be zoos and farms and docks and schools and space stations and much more. Encourage inventiveness. To stretch your child's imagination further, you might even ask him to build a structure representing an abstract concept—such as happiness, peace, or loneliness.

| ☑ Desire change and improvement | ☐ See a situation from a new perspective | ☐ Be willing to consider unusual and even absurd ideas | ☑ Take action to make improvements |

* Control Panels +

(what you need: paper, cardboard, markers, odds and ends)

Kids love control panels. Think of how their eyes light up when, for instance, they get to look inside the cockpit of an airplane.

This activity begins with a bit of imaginative discussion. Ask your child to imagine that she can invent a control panel that would allow her to operate and command people or events or other things that she otherwise couldn't. What would she like that control panel to do?

After you talk this over a while, give your child the supplies she needs to design such a panel. She can draw a relatively simple design on paper with pencil or markers, or she can create a more elaborate control panel on cardboard using markers and gluing on other items—buttons, rubber bands, paper clips, toothpicks—that will give the panel texture and three-dimensionality.

This activity encourages your child to be inventive. And the result will be a new item she can incorporate into her pretend play.

| ☑ Desire change and improvement | ☐ See a situation from a new perspective | ☑ Be willing to consider unusual and even absurd ideas | ☑ Take action to make improvements |

* Make a Game

(what you need: poster board, pieces of cardboard, crayons and markers, construction paper, scissors, large buttons, dice, old gift box)

As many toys or games as your child may have or think he wants, there's something exciting about creating a game from scratch. This activity places a premium on imagination—leave behind your adult sense of logic and structure, and a wonderful time is just about guaranteed.

Depending on the age and temperament of your child, you can merely present him with the items in the above list (the buttons make good game pieces) and tell him that there's a game waiting to be created in this pile of raw materials. It's up to him to imagine what it might be. Be sure to provide some scrap paper for testing ideas and designs.

> Leave behind your adult sense of logic, and a wonderful time is just about guaranteed.

Some children may need a bit of help. You might draw the snaking path that will take your child along the game's journey; you might discuss the concept of squares with special instructions; you might suggest creating a pile of cards to draw from for extra events within the game.

Once your child sinks into this activity, step back and let him be the master of the game's environment. Don't forget to have him design the box in which the game will be kept (that's what

| ☐ Desire change and improvement | ☑ See a situation from a new perspective | ☑ Be willing to consider unusual and even absurd ideas | ☑ Take action to make improvements |

the old gift box is for). As you play the game with your child, remember that the rules don't have to make sense and the game doesn't have to "work" in the way a packaged game does. Let him enjoy the process and have fun with it. No matter what else the game is, it will be unique.

* Chalk Town +

(what you need: sidewalk chalk, open blacktop or concrete area for drawing)

This is a great game if you have a private driveway. Kids certainly can have fun on their own with sidewalk chalk, but sometimes it helps to present them with a framework for their creativity.

Tell your child you would like her to draw a whole town on the driveway, complete with buildings and roads to connect them. To get her started, give her a list of a few buildings she might want to have in her town: a library, a gas station, a police station, a school, a museum, a movie theater, and so on. Have her think about which buildings she wants near other ones. Have her make the drawing big enough that she can ride her bicycle or pull a wagon around the town afterward.

For an extra twist, encourage some impossible additions—have her imagine and draw items in her town that could never be in a real town.

Just one word of caution: try not to suggest this game on a day when rain is expected or just before your automatic lawn sprinklers turn on. Your child may be disappointed to have her town "destroyed" that quickly.

☑ Desire change and improvement ☐ See a situation from a new perspective ☑ Be willing to consider unusual and even absurd ideas Take action to make improvements

* Ninas +

(what you need: paper, pens)

The caricature artist Al Hirschfeld has been making wonderful line drawings of actors and actresses in the *New York Times* for decades. One secret element of his drawings is that he always hides the word "Nina" among his penstrokes. He's been doing this ever since Nina—his daughter—was little. You can tell how many Ninas there are in the drawing by the number he puts next to his signature.

This hidden-word concept is the basis for a wonderful exercise in creative drawing. If you happen to have a copy of a Sunday *New York Times* Arts and Leisure section in which Hirschfeld has a drawing, show it to your child and find the Ninas together. If not, explain the basic concept. In either case, the point is to have your child make a drawing in which he hides a word in a few different places. In so doing, he is being forced to look at standard things in a nonstandard way. How, after all, can you draw a building so it hides a word?

You might have him start with Nina, for practice, because the simple up-and-down angles of the word in its upper-case form are relatively easy to blend into whatever might be in a drawing. But don't stop there. Have him do his own name or his sibling's. Or any other word that suits his fancy. Have him sign the drawing at the bottom and write a number to let you know how many hidden words to look for. And if you can't find all the words he has hidden, don't fret. With a little encouragement, your child may become a cartoonist in his own right.

| ☐ Desire change and improvement | ☑ See a situation from a new perspective | ☐ Be willing to consider unusual and even absurd ideas | ☐ Take action to make improvements |

MORE ARTS, CRAFTS, AND PROJECTS FOR 1ST AND 2ND GRADERS

(see Preschooler section)
- ☼ Coloring Box
- ☼ Scrambimals
- ☼ Crazycakes
- ☼ Brushless Painting

(see Kindergartner section)
- ☼ Bad Photographs
- ☼ Self-Portrait Dummy
- ☼ Progressive Art
- ☼ Alphabet Poster
- ☼ Fold-a-Creature

* Surreality

(what you need: spare photograph of your child; good quality paper, either white or colored; glue; markers or colored pencils)

Here's a wonderful older child's activity. Look through some family photographs together, find one she likes, and let her cut and glue.

Have her look at the picture she chooses and begin to think about a scene she might create, using all or part of the picture, that could never happen in real life. For instance, if the picture shows your child standing in winter clothing, she might think to cut off the lower legs, draw in a wild pair of space boots, and then create a scene around herself that suggests an adventure on a faraway planet.

Remind your child that the premise is to create a scene that could never really happen while at the same time incorporating the photograph as seamlessly—but inventively—as possible. Other than that, there are no rules and no guidelines. Colored pencils work well here, but thin markers are also fine. Encourage your child to spend a lot of thinking time on this one and to persevere until the scene is fully realized. This will be a creative work worth saving for enjoyment years later.

| ☑ Desire change and improvement | ☑ See a situation from a new perspective | ☑ Be willing to consider unusual and even absurd ideas | ☑ Take action to make improvements |

MORE ARTS, CRAFTS, AND PROJECTS FOR 3RD GRADERS AND OLDER

(see Preschooler section)
☆ Crazycakes

(see Kindergartner section)
☆ Bad Photographs
☆ Self-Portrait Dummy
☆ Progressive Art
☆ Fold-a-Creature

(see 1st and 2nd Grader section)
☆ Color Me Different
☆ Toothpick Architecture
☆ Control Panels
☆ Make a Game
☆ Chalk Town
☆ Ninas

CHAPTER SEVEN

Storytelling, Performance, and Fantasy

"Without imagination we are aimless."
—C.N. PARKINSON

Even in our high-tech, fast-paced, information-filled age, the ancient art of storytelling holds us rapt with its elegance, simplicity, and power. A skilled storyteller can still engage a child more deeply and fulfillingly than electronic bells and whistles.

The imagination is fueled by stories. Young children blossom creatively when given the time and encouragement not only to hear stories but also to invent them, tell and perform them, and improvise their own.

Television and other popular media have a place in a child's life, but parents hoping to raise truly creative and fulfilled children must be careful to see that their children have more stories in their lives than those provided by television, movies, and computer games. Many children seem unable to put even a two-sentence story together about their day at school and yet can reel off the complex details of a recently viewed television show without hesitation. Why are television's prefabricated, neatly wrapped stories more engaging than real life's more open-ended, unpackaged stories?

The answer lies in the question. Children raised to shy away from real life's complexities, whose imaginations have been too steadily contained and ordered by the entertainment business's stories, will grow with limited imaginations, and will be far less capable of creative thinking and creative responses to life.

The following activities are all ways to approach the same important task: how to nurture the art of storytelling in your child and, in so doing, nurture his or her creative spirit. Remember that a young child's lack of socially programmed inhibitions is one of his or her greatest creative gifts, and is particularly useful when telling stories, performing, and fantasizing. The activities in this section thrive on this freedom of expression and encourage all sorts of silliness and fun along the way.

* Secret Places +

Children love to have special, "secret" hiding places. Here's a chance for your child to discover one in her own house and maybe build a new one, too.

You might begin with a conversation about secret places. Ask your child the following: If she had a secret hiding place nobody knew about,

☆ what would it look like?

☆ what would she keep there?

☆ what would she do there?

Ask if she thinks there are any good secret hiding places in your house. Perhaps an idea will occur to her right away, perhaps not. Go on a secret hiding place hunt to discover one or more new places. She'll have fun looking at her everyday surroundings from a different perspective. Have her gather the special things she wants to keep in that hiding place. Don't forget the flashlight, which is a secret hiding place must.

If you have a card table, you can make a new hiding place on the spot with a blanket. Or use an old sheet, if you have one, and let your child cut out a door or window.

Remember:
Activities marked with a "+" are good for older children, too!

| ☑ Desire change and improvement | ☑ See a situation from a new perspective | ☐ Be willing to consider unusual and even absurd ideas | ☑ Take action to make improvements |

Another easily constructable secret place can be built using two chairs, two lengths of heavy string, and a sheet or a blanket. Set the chairs a few feet apart, back facing back, and connect them with the two strings. Then put a light blanket or a sheet over the string, pull the sides out like a tent, and hold them down with books at each corner.

Or let your child herself decide how to build a secret hiding place, stand back, and see what develops.

* Anti-Puppet Show +

(what you need: a box of assorted objects [see below])

Young children are naturally drawn to puppet shows, both as performers and as an audience. Many will duck behind a barrier at the drop of a hat to create a "show" for a parent, other family members, or friends.

While it's fun to have a bin of puppets ready to use for spontaneous productions, you can tweak your kids' creativity further by having them perform an anti-puppet show—a puppet show in which none of the puppets is an actual puppet.

If you normally keep puppets in one bin or box, remove the regular puppets and replace them with "anti-puppets." These can be puppet-like items such as old socks, oven mitts, or oversized mittens or gloves, or you can be really creative. An elastic bandage might work when wrapped around a child's wrist and hand. A paper bag. A towel. An old purse.

If your children are older and especially if more than one child is involved, all you will probably need to do is show them the bin with the anti-puppets and tell them to create an anti-puppet show. Let them know that you will come back to watch in, say, twenty minutes.

Younger children may need a bit more prompting, so put something silly on your own hand and create a character on the spot. Your child might respond by creating a character for the item he uses as a puppet (calling his puppet "Mr. Towel," for

| ✔ Desire change and improvement | ✔ See a situation from a new perspective | ✔ Be willing to consider unusual and even absurd ideas | ✔ Take action to make improvements |

example), or he might turn the item, imaginatively, into a more traditional puppet—transforming, say, a nine- by twelve-inch envelope into a puppy or a monkey. As usual, when it comes to creativity exercises, anything goes. Don't judge or cringe, just enjoy.

* Everybody Dance!

(what you need: toy musical instruments, bought or homemade ones)

Sit with your child in the midst of some musical instruments and explore the different noises each of them makes. Ask questions to help her listen carefully: Which instrument makes the loudest sound? Which makes the softest sound? Which makes the prettiest sound?

> **Loosen up and really move.**

You can then each take a turn playing the instruments. Have your child stand up and begin to move and dance in response to the sounds. Alter the rhythms and instruments, and see how your child reacts.

Then it's your turn to dance to your child's playing. Try to loosen up and really move. Make creative movements with your arms and legs and head and shoulders. Continue to alternate playing and dancing, and see how your child constantly improvises new movements.

| ☑ Desire change and improvement | ☐ See a situation from a new perspective | ☐ Be willing to consider unusual and even absurd ideas | ☑ Take action to make improvements |

* Singing the Day Away +

Here's a creative way to pass a few otherwise mundane household minutes. Tell your child that the two of you are going to begin singing everything you say to one another instead of talking. Demonstrate immediately by singing, "We are going to sing what we say to each other instead of talking! Do you have any questions?"

The more routine an activity you're doing at the time the better—whether getting a snack, making beds, or washing dishes. Don't think you can sing very well? No problem. Vocal quality is not a factor. Neither is the ability to construct anything like a "real" melody. Everyone gets an "A" for effort in this game. The point is to keep singing. You'll find some intriguing melodic recurrences and transformations begin to happen as you and your child play off each other.

Most of all, you'll be amazed how the apparently simple act of adding a melody to your words changes the whole tone of a routine activity. Smiles come quickly to faces, and suddenly everyone is having fun, not to mention looking at the mundane, everyday world in an entirely new way.

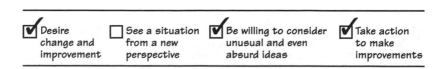

| ☑ Desire change and improvement | ☐ See a situation from a new perspective | ☑ Be willing to consider unusual and even absurd ideas | ☑ Take action to make improvements |

* The Magic Corner +

Pick out a corner in your house where you can sit comfortably while your child easily disappears around it. Tell your child this is a magic corner, and whoever goes around it counts to three and comes back as a different person or character.

You can demonstrate by having him sit while you turn the corner, count to three, and then come back as, say, a witch or a clown or whatever else occurs to you. Use large gestures and exaggerated vocal tones to help create your character; with older children, you might want to offer this as a helpful hint. An older child who knows a little about the theater may also be told to think of this as an imaginary, super-fast costume change—each time he goes around the corner, he's taking off one costume and putting on another. Younger children seem to have no problem catching on, and while their character "changes" may not be too obvious to an observer, they will go about their business merrily and without question.

If your child needs prompting, you can offer suggestions during his three count. If he has plenty of ideas, you can turn it into a game in which you try to guess who he is each time he comes back.

You can expand the activity by moving to a different corner and pretending that this one has a different power—perhaps it turns your child into animals or prompts a new emotion or changes how he walks each time he goes around and comes back. If your child really enjoys this activity, perhaps he will discover something magical about *every* corner in your house.

| ☐ Desire change and improvement | ☑ See a situation from a new perspective | ☑ Be willing to consider unusual and even absurd ideas | ☐ Take action to make improvements |

* Name That Sound +

Our world is full of sounds. Children are more attuned to them than adults, as you're about to see.

This activity will work inside or outside, but not in an indoor public area, since there's no predicting what sounds will emerge from your child in the process. Ask her to think of a sound she hears every day, and then have her attempt to imitate it with her voice. You can start with obvious sounds like a car going by or a tea kettle whistling, but guide her toward less commonly imitated noises, such as the refrigerator humming, a light switch being turned on or off, or the sound of shoes walking across a wooden floor.

You might start with sounds you can actually hear or create on the spot. After a few of those, you can move to noises that do not come from the immediate environment. Take turns making the sounds. You can play this as a guessing game, where you try to guess what sound the other person is making, or simply as a creative exercise.

Feel free to expand the game into the realm of sound effects by employing everyday objects to help create a desired noise. Then add an extra, creative spin by moving into a purely imaginary world. Ask your child to invent a noise, and then you can invent whatever it is that might be making that noise. Then you can invent a noise and have your child decide what the noise is. Or do it in reverse: create a description first—such as, "The sound bricks make when they talk to each other" or "The sound a Martian makes when it washes its face"—and then concoct the sound. In this version, silliness is definitely encouraged.

| ☐ Desire change and improvement | ☑ See a situation from a new perspective | ☑ Be willing to consider unusual and even absurd ideas | ☐ Take action to make improvements |

* Instant Animals

When children are still learning animal sounds, they love having the opportunity to "perform" them. This quick little game is just the stage they need.

Cover your face with your hands and say, "Show me a pussycat!" Then uncover your face, which is your child's cue to act like a pussycat with his voice and his body. After a few seconds, cover your face again and say, "Show me a duck!" Once more uncover your face and watch your child be a duck.

Keep the pace quick but not too quick—be sure to share in your child's obvious delight at acting out so many wonderful parts.

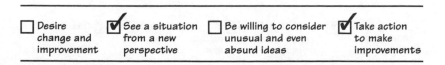

☐ Desire   ☑ See a situation   ☐ Be willing to consider   ☑ Take action
change and   from a new   unusual and even   to make
improvement   perspective   absurd ideas   improvements

* Story Retelling +

Your child should be well used to hearing stories from you by now. Here's a chance to let her tell you a story.

You can do this as you are about to read her a story. Perhaps you've already pulled a particularly favorite book from the shelf. This time instead of reading the book, open it in front of your child and have her "read" it to you herself. The fact that she can't read is not likely to stop her—most children will launch into the story with little prompting. If she seems to need help starting, remind her of the first sentence. You may be amazed how much she remembers, and even how much inflection she uses in her voice, in imitation of yours.

> **Let your child tell you a story.**

If your child is older, let her finish the story the original way, then have her go back and give the story a different ending. Even though she may have heard the story told the "right way" a hundred times, she'll probably have no trouble creating a new ending for an old book.

☑ Desire change and improvement ☑ See a situation from a new perspective ☑ Be willing to consider unusual and even absurd ideas ☑ Take action to make improvements

STORYTELLING, PERFORMANCE, AND FANTASY FOR KINDERGARTNERS

* Story Deck +

(what you need: old magazines and catalogs, scissors, index cards, glue)

This is a multifaceted activity that can be replayed over and over. With your child, begin by looking through a stack of old magazines and catalogs and choosing pictures to cut out. The pictures don't have to be the same size and don't have to be perfectly cut; the only requirement is that they fit onto index cards (four- by six-inch cards will allow larger pictures, of course). If you have any sort of an "interesting pictures" file, pull this out, too, and choose some of those pictures.

When you have a good number of pictures (you can start with a dozen or so, but older children may want as many as twenty or even more), glue each one to its own index card. Turn them over, shuffle them, and place them in a pile face down in front of you. Have your child turn over the top card. This is where your story begins.

What your child will do is create a story, using each picture that you turn over as a guide. He may need a bit of help from you at first. If he first turns over a picture of a car, you might suggest starting with, "Once upon a time, there was a magic car, and whoever got behind the wheel could drive instantly to anywhere in the solar system."

He then turns over the next card and takes it as a cue for the next bit of the story, and so forth. You can allow him to tell the

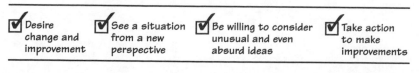

| ✓ Desire change and improvement | ✓ See a situation from a new perspective | ✓ Be willing to consider unusual and even absurd ideas | ✓ Take action to make improvements |

whole story, with assistance from you, or you can take turns adding to the story. The Story Deck works especially well with a couple of children and one or two adults, with everyone taking a turn drawing a card and adding to the story.

When you get down to the last few cards, announce it so the storyteller or storytellers know they must soon come to an end. The person who draws the last card has the challenge of wrapping up the story in whatever weird and wonderful way he can think of. Loose ends are not only fine but encouraged. Anything goes, even the clichéd but ever-useful, "And Billy woke up and realized it was all a dream!"

Once you've gone through the deck, shuffle it and begin again. A whole new story will emerge, but don't be surprised if your child borrows a lot of ideas and events from the first story. Allow him to build the story however he sees fit, while you encourage experimentation and new tangents through your own additions.

* Junk Bin Sort +

(what you need: a household "junk" bin)

Everybody has a basket or bin or drawer somewhere in which all stray items seem to end up. Birthday party favors, lost pieces from forgotten games, unwanted baseball cards, partially broken toy cars: they all end up in the junk bin.

This activity can begin like an older child's version of the "Categories" activity listed in the "Arts, Crafts, and Projects" chapter. Take everything in the junk bin or drawer and dump it on the floor. (Be sure to remove any items with sharp edges.) Tell your child that you're going to leave the room while she sorts through the junk and groups everything into just three or four categories of her invention. Then you'll come back and see if you can guess what the categories are. After doing it once, see if she can do it again using three new categories.

When she's ready for a new challenge, have her select an item from each of the categories and put them aside. (Now we are about to turn this into a sort of three-dimensional version of the Story Deck.) Ask her to make up a story that involves these three items. It can be a story with an end, or it can be a story that has to be continued, in which case you can then choose three items and continue the story yourself. Then it's her turn again, and so on.

A good way to wind the story down is to include reasons why each piece of "junk" has to "go home"—that is, be returned to the bin from which it came. This way, if all goes well, when the story is over, everything is cleaned up, too.

☐ Desire change and improvement   ☑ See a situation from a new perspective   ☑ Be willing to consider unusual and even absurd ideas   ☑ Take action to make improvements

* Mirror Mirror +

Sit or stand facing your child, and decide who is going to be the mirror first. The person who is the mirror must copy the actions of the other person (the "performer"). Start with slow, simple movements. As you both grow accustomed to your roles, the performer should begin to use different body parts. While motions should not be abrupt or quick, they should grow more complex and surprising. (Remember the classic comedy routine in which Lucille Ball mirrored Harpo Marx?)

Switch roles often. Encourage unexpected movements, appreciate creativity, and if you're not laughing soon you're taking the activity a little too seriously.

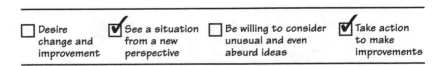

| ☐ Desire change and improvement | ☑ See a situation from a new perspective | ☐ Be willing to consider unusual and even absurd ideas | ☑ Take action to make improvements |

MORE STORYTELLING, PERFORMANCE, AND FANTASY FOR KINDERGARTNERS

(see Preschooler section)
- ☼ Secret Places
- ☼ Anti-Puppet Show
- ☼ Singing the Day Away
- ☼ The Magic Corner
- ☼ Name That Sound
- ☼ Story Retelling

* People Factory +

(what you need: three small paper bags, scrap paper, pen or pencil)

Simple yet multifaceted, easy to catch on to yet highly involving—the People Factory beats them all in creating fun for a wide range of ages.

Start with three small paper bags and label them "first,"

> Guide your child toward unexpected territory with thought-provoking questions.

"middle," and "last." Rip the scrap paper into about thirty small rectangles, each just big enough to write one name on. Sit down with your child and explain that the two of you are going to come up with an assortment of first,

middle, and last names for imaginary characters.

The goal is to devise names that are silly yet evocative and somehow at least vaguely name-like. You can decide to do all the first names first, then the middle names, then the last names, or you can simply create some names and decide on the spot which bag they belong in. Allow your child free rein, but work with him to model a good mix of names—invent a few that sound somehow happy (Crinklestomper?), a few that sound downright villainous (Blotfester?), and a whole bunch of generally fun and funny-sounding monikers (Harbfarfle, Wooshwallower, Frump). Mix some real, if slightly uncom-

| ☐ Desire change and improvement | ☐ See a situation from a new perspective | ☑ Be willing to consider unusual and even absurd ideas | ☐ Take action to make improvements |

mon, names in for variety (Priscilla, Egbert, Thaddeus). If you come up short, feel free to add some of your favorite literary names (Fezziwigg is always popular) in the last name bag, and don't forget to mix in some simple initials (J. and T. work especially well) in both the "first" and "middle" bags.

Once there are at least ten names in each bag, it's time to manufacture a few people. Have your child pick one first, one middle, and one last name and put them together. Have him say the name a couple of times. Then ask him to imagine what this person might be like. You can begin with a simple physical description—is he tall or short, young or old, fat or thin? Guide your child toward more unexpected territory with thought-provoking questions like

- What kind of job does this person have?
- Would you be friends with this person? Why or why not?
- If you had to spend an afternoon with this person, what would you do?
- What does this person like to watch on television?

Younger children may, after a little bit of description, want to choose a new name. Older children should be encouraged to create a reasonably full character before moving on to another. If you can play with two or more children, it's fun to let them create three or four characters and then put them together in a story or a play. You might even consider bringing out the video camera for the end result, to capture a bit of J. Bleeber Hulahoop for posterity.

* Grand-story +

(paper and pencil optional, but encouraged)

This is a scene-setting story game based on a real character: one of your child's grandparents or, better yet, great-grandparents, if any are still alive. Begin a discussion about how different life was for this grandparent or great-grandparent when he or she was your child's age. See how many things your child can list that were different, from obvious things like there being no television to less obvious things like what foods were eaten back then. Prompt your child to think about what kind of house the grandparent might have lived in, what sort of jobs his or her mother and father had, what type of school he or she went to, and what sorts of activities everyone did for fun.

Once you've established the setting with some detail, have your child begin a story that attempts to tell about a day in the life of the grandparent as a child. Encourage your child to wonder out loud about details she might not know. Have her think about, and even write down, specific questions that she might want to ask this grandparent directly, such as, "What kind of food did you keep in your pantry?" or "What was the first movie you ever saw?"

After your child has imagined what her grandparent's typical day was like, you might write down the story together and send it in a letter to the grandparent. Tell him or her how the

| ☐ Desire change and improvement | ☑ See a situation from a new perspective | ☐ Be willing to consider unusual and even absurd ideas | ☐ Take action to make improvements |

story was written and express interest in learning more details from that time gone by. Include the questions that arose during the imagining of the story.

When the grandparent writes back, you can use this response to begin another story, employing new details and fresh bits of imagination to begin a new tale.

* The Prop Box +

(what you need: a large box of assorted objects)

This activity works best with an audience—either you watching your child, a few kids together, or a bunch of kids and parents. And it does require a bit of work in advance: collecting a good number of household objects into one container. They can be almost anything—a dustpan, a combination lock, a yardstick, a tube of toothpaste, a shoe box—but it pays to have a good assortment of sizes and shapes. Look in the basement for some real finds—a large forgotten basket, an extra pair of safety goggles, or unneeded vacuum cleaner attachments.

Begin by handing your child, or the first "performer," a prop and have him act out as many creative routines ("riffs," as they say in show business) with it as possible. The point is to use the prop in ways it wasn't meant to be used. He might take the dustpan, for instance, and use it as a fly-swatter. Then a hair brush. Then a fan. He might sit at a table and use it as a quill pen or prance around the room as a peacock, with the dustpan as his tail.

The routines can be short or more involved; they can be pantomimes or your child can speak. Anything goes. Encourage using one prop in as many ways as possible. Move on to the next prop only when he has literally run out of ideas.

| ✓ Desire change and improvement | ✓ See a situation from a new perspective | ✓ Be willing to consider unusual and even absurd ideas | ✓ Take action to make improvements |

If there are a few children, you might begin by giving each a prop and then allowing them to do one routine each, in a circle, until they begin to run out of ideas. Or, after each has done a few riffs on the first prop, have everyone pass the prop to the person on the left and start again.

MORE STORYTELLING, PERFORMANCE, AND FANTASY FOR 1ST AND 2ND GRADERS

(see Preschooler section)
⚝ Secret Places
⚝ Anti-Puppet Show
⚝ Singing the Day Away
⚝ The Magic Corner
⚝ Name That Sound
⚝ Story Retelling

(see Kindergartner section)
⚝ Story Deck
⚝ Junk Bin Sort
⚝ Mirror Mirror

STORYTELLING, PERFORMANCE, AND FANTASY FOR
3RD GRADERS AND OLDER

* Day-by-Day Story

(what you need: blank notebook; pen or pencil; crayons [optional])

Here's a creativity-nurturing tool that takes almost no time on any given day. Because the result is revealed slowly, this is an especially good exercise to nourish perseverance, to show concretely how worthwhile projects sometimes take a lot of time.

Begin with a blank notebook. If your child writes easily, have her write on the first page, "My Day-by-Day Story" and her name. Have her also write the date on which she begins the story.

> Here's a creativity-nurturing tool that takes almost no time.

The only rule here is that your child must write just one sentence a day. This may be difficult at first, but the discipline of it will grow easier over time. If your child enjoys drawing, you can encourage her to illustrate the story as it develops. The final product will be a surprise to everyone and will clearly show the value of staying with a project over time.

When the story is done, have the whole family gather for its first telling. Let your child sit as a storyteller does, facing her audience, and give her a big round of applause when she finishes.

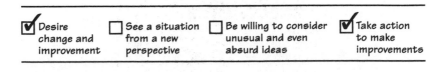

| ☑ Desire change and improvement | ☐ See a situation from a new perspective | ☐ Be willing to consider unusual and even absurd ideas | ☑ Take action to make improvements |

MORE STORYTELLING, PERFORMANCE, AND FANTASY FOR 3RD GRADERS AND OLDER

(see Preschooler section)
   ☆ Story Retelling

(see Kindergartner section)
   ☆ Story Deck
   ☆ Junk Bin Sort

(see 1st and 2nd Grader section)
   ☆ People Factory
   ☆ Grand-story
   ☆ The Prop Box

CHAPTER EIGHT

Creative Experiences

"Grown-ups never understand anything for themselves. . . . Children [are] always and forever explaining things to them."

—ANTOINE DE SAINT-EXUPERY

Sometimes you can have the most wonderful creativity-enhancing moments with children in a real-world context. Never mind the set-up, the arts and crafts materials, or even the elaborate, imaginative premises. All these next activities require is an observant eye and a sense of wonder. The question is, Do you, as an adult, have what it takes?

You know what? You do. Watch your kids. Learn from them. Have fun.

CREATIVE EXPERIENCES FOR PRESCHOOLERS

* Yucky Day Hike +

Sometimes, creativity is nurtured by a simple but powerfully counterintuitive suggestion. For instance, when, in the middle of watching a torrential downpour on the kind of day that no sane person would voluntarily venture outside, you matter-of-factly decide it's time for a walk.

It becomes interesting to realize that you really can dress appropriately even for a downpour. Spacious raincoats, snug boots, old pants, and a broad umbrella will do the trick. You don't have to walk very far to revel in the novelty of being outside in such weather. Point out the wonderful noises the rain makes on umbrellas, hoods, streets, mailboxes, and cars. Find inviting puddles to splash in; there is hardly a child on the planet who is not instinctively creative when faced with serious splashing puddles. And think of all the things you get to see by being outside that people who stay inside might never know about.

You don't have to stay out for very long. Even after ten minutes of this wild weather adventure, you'll return invigorated and refreshed. And the day won't look so dreary after all.

Remember:
Activities marked with a "+" are good for older children, too!

| ☐ Desire change and improvement | ☐ See a situation from a new perspective | ☑ Be willing to consider unusual and even absurd ideas | ☑ Take action to make improvements |

* Cloud Watching +

This is surely one of humankind's oldest imaginative games. It's such a classic that it's not only easy to forget, it's also easy to overlook how perfectly suited a simple round of cloud watching can be to developing creativity.

Find a comfortable place to lie down and gaze at the sky. The best way to let your child's imagination run free is to keep your comments open-ended. That is, try not to ask something like, "Do you see the elephant?" It's better simply to say, with enthusiasm, "Wow! Look at that big cloud! What do you think it looks like?" Then listen as your child's imagination takes off.

| ☐ Desire change and improvement | ☑ See a situation from a new perspective | ☑ Be willing to consider unusual and even absurd ideas | ☐ Take action to make improvements |

* Take Out!

(what you need: a shelf in a cabinet or pantry with child-friendly packages)

Your children see you going into the pantry every day for things you need, taking them out, then returning them. Once a child is old enough to stand and remove things from a shelf in your pantry, she may love the opportunity to take out small boxes and cans and return them in her own fashion, according to her own unique sense of order.

> You can increase your child's play experience by asking questions.

This activity needs little direction or guidance. Children seem to know just what to do and love the opportunity to play with real food. You can increase your child's play experience by asking questions about what she's "buying," what she's planning to make for dinner, who's coming over to eat, and so on. At the same time, you can begin to introduce your young child to creative behavior modeling by having her assemble, say, a dinner made up entirely of things that aren't usually for dinner, such as oatmeal with chocolate syrup. And if you're feeling *really* creative, you can even help your "little chef" cook up her unique meal.

| ☐ Desire change and improvement | ☑ See a situation from a new perspective | ☑ Be willing to consider unusual and even absurd ideas | ☐ Take action to make improvements |

* Backyard Soup +

(what you need: a big pot filled with water, a spoon, a nice day)

Find a large, sturdy pot that you won't mind getting a bit dirty, and fill it two-thirds full of water. Tell your child it's time to make backyard soup and you need his help.

Backyard soup, you explain, is a magical concoction that tastes like nothing else in the world. It is made with natural things you find in the backyard and must be properly stirred and tended as it "cooks." (This activity requires children who have a clear sense of pretend; if there's any chance your child will think he's really able to eat the soup, he's not old enough for this one.)

Set the pot on the lawn in the backyard and let your child hunt for "ingredients." Encourage small quantities at any one time—two or three leaves, for instance, instead of an armful. Remind him, if necessary, that ingredients must be smaller than the cooking pot. Make sure he remembers to stir his creation as he goes. Ask him every now and then how it smells and when it'll be ready. If he wants, you can "serve" it in small plastic sand buckets or old margarine tubs—you can even spread out a blanket, invite some stuffed animals, and have a soup party. Sounds good, doesn't it?

| ☑ Desire change and improvement | ☑ See a situation from a new perspective | ☑ Be willing to consider unusual and even absurd ideas | ☑ Take action to make improvements |

**CREATIVE EXPERIENCES FOR
KINDERGARTNERS**

* Strange Shadows +

(what you need: sidewalk chalk, sunny day)

With the sun at a height in the sky that creates a good shadow on the ground, take your child to a blacktop area along with a few big pieces of sidewalk chalk.

Stand so that your shadow falls on a flat stretch of blacktop. Have your child trace your shadow to the best of her ability. Next, move a few steps over to one side and have your child

| ☑ Desire change and improvement | ☑ See a situation from a new perspective | ☑ Be willing to consider unusual and even absurd ideas | ☑ Take action to make improvements |

draw your shadow again, but enhanced somehow. Perhaps she'll want to give you a head like a space alien, a tail like a dragon, six legs, or anything else either of you can think of.

You can take turns doing this activity—your child may get a big kick out of stepping into her own strange shadow. Besides, it's always good to keep your own creativity on its toes.

* New Holidays

(what you need: pencil and paper, spare calendar)

Kids love holidays. Why not give them a chance to create their own?

Have your child begin a list of holidays he'd like to invent. Make it a real brainstorm session, with no idea too strange or outlandish. Peanut Butter Day? Sure. Silly Walk Day? Why not. Older children may want to take the concept more seriously. How about Inventors' Day to celebrate great inventions in human history? Or Money Day, when we count our money and roll up spare change?

Once he has a list going, he can decide where on the calendar his holidays belong. He can also decide upon their relative importance. Which holidays should involve closing schools, banks, and post offices? From among all the new holidays, have him choose one to create in greater detail. How will people celebrate it? Will they wear special clothes to commemorate the day? What might people give to one another on this holiday? What songs might be sung in observance? What foods will be eaten?

Once the holiday is thoroughly conceived, you can add an extra touch to the activity by having your child create a card wishing the recipient a Happy _____ Day (filling in the name of the new holiday), and have him send it to a grandparent with a little note of explanation.

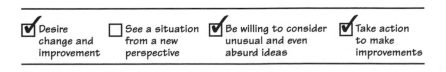

| ✔ Desire change and improvement | ☐ See a situation from a new perspective | ✔ Be willing to consider unusual and even absurd ideas | ✔ Take action to make improvements |

* Around the House

(what you need: stopwatch, or watch with a second hand)

Here's a good cure for cabin fever, in almost any weather. Dress your child (and yourself!) appropriately (paying extra attention to footgear), head outside, and tell her she's going to race around the house and you're going to time her. Most kindergartners love to be timed.

But that's just the beginning. Once she arrives at the finish line, tell her this time you want her to go around the house galloping like a horse. Time her again. (You don't have to "do" anything with these times, simply announce them with great enthusiasm.) The next time, have her walk backwards. Or hop every other step. Or walk with extra long strides. As we often say in this book, anything goes. After a few times around, she will probably begin to suggest new ways to walk around the house.

This activity doesn't have to go on for too long, especially in inclement weather. After a half-dozen or so trips around the house, your little wacky racer should be ready for a nice cup of hot chocolate. Make one for yourself, too.

| ☐ Desire change and improvement | ☐ See a situation from a new perspective | ☑ Be willing to consider unusual and even absurd ideas | ☑ Take action to make improvements |

MORE CREATIVE EXPERIENCES FOR KINDERGARTNERS

(see Preschooler section)
- ☼ Yucky Day Hike
- ☼ Cloud Watching
- ☼ Backyard Soup

CREATIVE EXPERIENCES FOR
1ST AND 2ND GRADERS

* Map Your World +

(what you need: pencil and paper)

Can you teach your child a bit about spatial relationships, foster creativity, and have fun at the same time? You bet.

Begin in your child's room with a blank piece of paper and a pencil. Sketch a rectangle to represent the walls of the room, label the paper "_____'s Room" (with your child's name in the blank space), and then draw the shape of something large that's in his room, like the bed or a dresser. Show your child how you've drawn it on the map in the same place the actual object is in his room. Now ask him where some other substantial item in the room would be if you were to draw it on the map—the door or the window, perhaps. Then add it to the map as well, or depending on the age of your child, have him do it.

Keep going until the whole room is mapped. You can check to see how well he's catching on to the concept by finding something small to use as a treasure, hiding it in the room, and indicating on the map where it can be found.

At this point, the game can be spun in a couple of directions. You can have your child think of a favorite character from a story or a nursery rhyme and have him create a map of what this character's room might look like. Or you can have him pre-

| ☐ Desire change and improvement | ☑ See a situation from a new perspective | ☑ Be willing to consider unusual and even absurd ideas | ☑ Take action to make improvements |

tend that animals have rooms like people and see what he might create for a cat or a rabbit or a zebra.

Then take the concept a different place. Talk about how the rooms he has been creating all come from his imagination. Tell him a person's imagination is a magical place full of mysterious and wonderful ideas and thoughts. Ask him then to make a map of his imagination. What does he imagine is there—lots of closets and shelves and drawers? Stacks of books? Hidden hallways and secret passages? Encourage small details and whimsical conjectures. Bring out some crayons or markers to add color. You'll be so fascinated with the results, you'll probably want to map your imagination, too.

Introducing Imagination

While parents should avoid turning play into lessons or lectures, some experts believe that young children should be introduced to the idea of imagination as they first gain a mastery of language and ideas.

You might begin by telling your child that there is something inside his head that he can't see, but it helps him to think of things no one else can think of. This something in his head is called imagination. Make the concept concrete by reminding him of something he's thought of, an idea he's had, or a game he's invented.

Reinforce the concept any time you and your child engage in a creative activity by encouraging him to take his time and use his imagination. And always be appreciative of any and all imaginative efforts with a simple, "That's using your imagination!"

* Art Tales +

(what you need: an art museum)

Many adults don't think of an art museum as a place to take small children—perhaps because too many of us have less than pleasant memories of being dragged through such a place when we were young, ready to collapse out of sheer boredom after just a few minutes.

If a child becomes bored when an adult takes her into art museums, it's because the adult has not attempted to see the art from a child's point of view. Children are actually quite ready to be captivated by all kinds of art if prompted by the right questions.

> **Children are quite ready to be captivated by art.**

You can begin by having your child simply pick out her favorite painting on a given wall or in a given room. Once she chooses one, ask her why she likes it, and accept any explanation as an answer. Encourage your child to talk about how the painting makes her feel and why. Find visually interesting elements in it yourself and discuss them, whether it's the intensity of a color, the texture of the brushstrokes, the realism of a landscape, or the geometry of an abstraction. Ask her what she might want to change about the painting and why.

Another way to engage your child in a museum is to pick a painting and turn it into a story. A boat on the ocean can

☐ Desire change and improvement	☑ See a situation from a new perspective	☐ Be willing to consider unusual and even absurd ideas	☐ Take action to make improvements

become a magical journey by a brave princess in search of a legendary golden dragon. A green meadow scene is transformed into a hiding place for bandits and thieves. An abstract layout of swirls and wiggles becomes what the sky looks like on a new planet or a magician's dream or what it feels like to have a surprise party.

* It's a Big/Small World After All +

(what you need: clipboard and paper or pad, pencil)

Children can be instantly engaged when asked to train their considerable powers of observation in unexpected ways. This activity turns their sometimes too-familiar house into a new environment awaiting discovery.

Tell your child he must conduct a household search for the biggest and smallest objects in a certain category. You can either suggest a category—books, stuffed animals, or plants— or prepare a number of categories in advance, write each on a sheet of paper, and put them all in a bag from which your child can pick.

Write the name of the category on a sheet of paper, with the words "big" and "small" listed underneath, and send him on his search. A younger child might want to look for the big thing separately from the small thing, while older children might want to write down more than one category at a time and search for the big and small items simultaneously.

While younger children will have fun with simple categories, older children will welcome the challenge of trying to find less common objects. The more unusual the category, the more creative your child will have to be.

| ☐ Desire change and improvement | ☑ See a situation from a new perspective | ☑ Be willing to consider unusual and even absurd ideas | ☐ Take action to make improvements |

* Super Duper Game +

(what you need: construction paper, markers, cardboard, old magazines, glue stick, dice, old shoe box)

This may look like an art project, but it's actually more of a full-fledged creative happening. Still, you need a few supplies, as you can see. The end result is a game in which the "board" is as big as or even bigger than a room.

Begin by cutting the construction paper into six reasonably equal rectangles. You can start with fifty rectangles, although your child may ultimately want to increase the number to seventy-five or one hundred. If your child is old enough to cut straight lines, definitely have her help. After the rectangles are cut, work together to number them consecutively. Then take one more sheet of construction paper, cut it in half, and label one half "Start" and the other half "Finish."

(Feel free to encourage more creative shapes or more elaborate decorating. But be aware that anything involving this many pieces could lose a child's interest before the game actually starts.)

Next, go through old magazines to locate a few pictures that would make good "tokens" for the game. Cut out three or four and glue them to a piece of cardboard for sturdiness.

Now it's time for your child to take over. Have her lay out a "game board" by placing the numbered rectangles on the floor in any design she likes. (Just be sure she does it in a room or rooms in the house you don't mind her playing in for a while—

| ☑ Desire change and improvement | ☑ See a situation from a new perspective | ☑ Be willing to consider unusual and even absurd ideas | ☑ Take action to make improvements |

maybe the playroom, maybe the kitchen, or maybe both.) She might set up a long straight line or a big oblong or a wavy path. Maybe she wants the path to end up where it started, or maybe she wants it to end around two different corners. Once the design is completed, have her place the "Start" and "Finish" rectangles in the appropriate places.

(At some time in the creation process, you might point out the shoe box to your child and inform her that that's where the game will be stored when you're done—that she must help clean it up. It's always good to tell children about this in advance.)

Now choose a token, and the game begins. You can make the game relatively simple: just move along by rolling the dice and see who gets to the end first. Or make up extra rules: if one person lands on the other person's token, she sends the first person back (to the start, for example); perhaps something interesting will happen if you roll doubles; or add elements your child comes up with. There is a lot of room for creativity here, and then there's just the basic fun of moving a marker around such a big "board." This activity is a real event and will happily involve your child for quite a long time.

**MORE CREATIVE EXPERIENCES FOR
1ST AND 2ND GRADERS**

(see Preschooler section)
- ☀ Yucky Day Hike
- ☀ Cloud Watching

(see Kindergartner section)
- ☀ Strange Shadows
- ☀ New Holidays
- ☀ Around the House

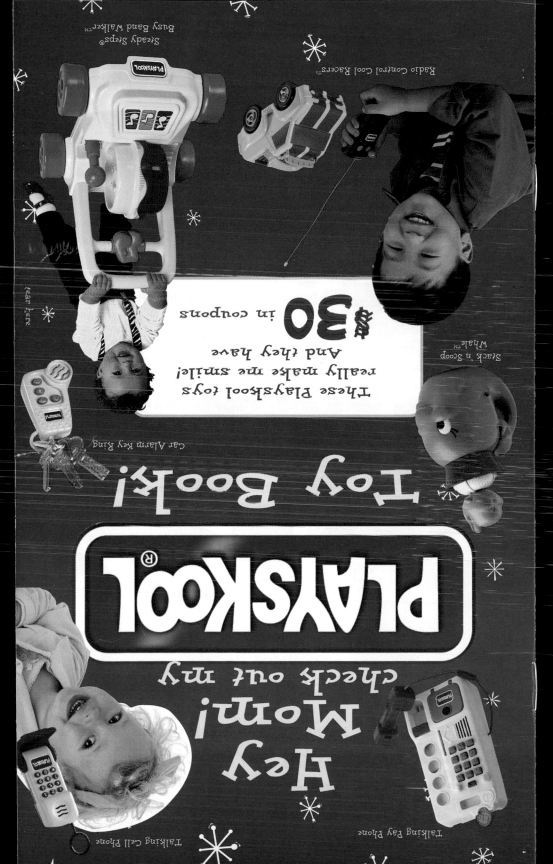

PLAYSKOOL

Rockin' Radio®

Talking Barney®

Gloworm®

Talking Arthur™

**CREATIVE EXPERIENCES FOR
3RD GRADERS AND OLDER**

* Kitchen Sink Game

(what you need: "orphaned" boards and pieces from games no one uses anymore, large shoe box)

While we're on the subject of unusual and creative games, here's a chance for your child to rejuvenate old games that might have been sitting in the "throw out someday" heap.

First, have him go on a hunt with you for old games—games that are never played, games that have missing pieces, games that your children have outgrown. Make sure he agrees that these games are otherwise unusable, then let him know that he can bring them back to life.

> A new game is your child's to invent.

Begin by taking the game boards and, if there is more than one, putting them in a pile. Then have your child gather all the different pieces, tokens, cards, play money, and whatever else is in the various boxes and put them all in the shoe box. Tell him to close the lid and shake the pieces up, just to be sure that they're all mixed up and ready for a whole new life. If he wants, he can add any other incomplete sets of cards, dominoes, dice, toy animals, or play money he has lying around his room—or any other small things (old birthday party favors are good for this) that have been sitting in a corner or a drawer for longer than anyone can remember.

☑ Desire change and improvement ☑ See a situation from a new perspective ☑ Be willing to consider unusual and even absurd ideas ☑ Take action to make improvements

Now the fun begins. A new game is his to invent, or even a series of games. If he needs prompting, go over a few basics that all games usually share:

- a start and a finish
- pieces that move around a board
- pictures on the board
- a counter (such as dice or a spinner)
- rewards and penalties (that is, lucky and unlucky things that happen when you land on a certain spot, spin a certain number, or pick a certain card)
- a way to win

Or scrap conventional structure entirely and let your child reimagine the whole concept of a game.

Create a new game board using one of the old boards. Your child can either draw directly on it to change and augment what's there, or he can cover it up entirely with paper and draw his own path and pictures.

Encourage experimentation and change. If there is more than one game board, have him try a whole different design and concept. When he has a game ready, set a time for you to play it together. Once it works to his satisfaction, have him name it, write down the rules, and design a new box for it. This is one game that won't get put on the shelf and be forgotten.

MORE CREATIVE EXPERIENCES FOR 3RD GRADERS AND OLDER

(see Kindergartner section)
- ☆ Strange Shadows
- ☆ New Holidays

(see 1st and 2nd Grader section)
- ☆ Map Your World
- ☆ Art Tales
- ☆ It's a Big/Small World After All
- ☆ Super Duper Game

PART THREE

Creativity and the World Beyond

CHAPTER NINE

The Media Menagerie

"Looking for ideas is like prospecting for gold.
If you look in the same old places, you'll find tapped
out veins. . . . Venture off the beaten path."

—UNKNOWN

During every waking hour, we are surrounded by electronic media: televisions bring us news and entertainment, computers help many of us work and play.

Not only do they surround us, they seem ever intent on increasing their roles in our lives through technological innovation. Just as the VCR expanded our sense of what a television could do in the 1980s, vastly increasing its utility and entertainment value, so is the World Wide Web currently expanding our sense of what the computer can do in the 1990s and beyond. And a number of other new technologies appear poised in the wings, including high-definition television (HDTV), Web television, digital video discs (DVD), and more.

As ubiquitous as the television and the computer are, some people use them more than others, of course. As an adult, how much time you spend watching television or glued to the computer screen is your own business.

Children, however, are not adults. Children are people whose brains and thought patterns are in the early stages of development. Excessive exposure to the images and sounds streaming from our electronic media can have a dire effect on a child's imagination and creativity.

There's nothing wrong with children watching television or using a computer per se. Problems arise, however, when it comes to time and content: how long kids watch and what they watch.

Working with Television

The television and the computer are entrenched in our daily lives. Parents should be aware of the dangers of overexposure, but just because a lot of television may be bad for kids doesn't mean that the only appropriate path is no television at all. A little moderation goes a long way.

As parents, we know we should be careful about what our children watch and the sorts of games they play. We are told, in fact, to watch television with our children whenever possible and to talk together about the programs.

There is a lot of creativity-enhancing potential in this idea. You can talk directly about the shows, asking questions about the situations presented, the choices characters made, how real or unreal the show was. But you can also take it a step further and use the content of the show, or the computer game, as a springboard for imaginative discussions. If you just finished watching a cartoon in which action heroes saved the world (yet again), you can ask your child what values he thinks are worth protecting in the world and talk about real-life, nonviolent ways that people can protect them.

By extending the conversation beyond screen time, you can understand what your child is enthusiastic about on the screen and then use that enthusiasm to guide thought and creativity beyond what is passively received.

The time issue is pretty simple: time spent watching television or using a computer—let's call it "screen time"—is time spent not doing other things that are important to the healthy development of a young mind and body. Children parked in front of a screen are not moving their bodies, getting fresh air, or exercising their imaginations or intellects.

This last point is especially important when it comes to creativity. When television replaces play time, this is no idle substitution. According to child development experts, play is not just nice or appropriate for children; it is a crucial part of the way children learn, develop, and grow. There is little chance for creativity to flourish in a play-deprived child.

But there's even more to the problem than play deprivation. Television delivers a fast-paced, prepackaged environment that offers not even the slightest clue to children about how they are to think. Even so-called educational programs are oriented toward a high-speed progression of images and words. They provide children with information but very rarely invite or foster genuine thinking.

Watching television is, furthermore, a pale substitute for the genuinely creative acts of both listening to stories and telling them. Children are all too able to recite the details of a recently watched sitcom, while they are typically incapable of shaping a story out of an event that happened to them in real life only a few hours earlier.

This is no idle philosophical musing. There is physiological evidence to indicate that overexposure to "second-hand images"—that is, moving images that originate from an outside source, rather than from within a child's imagination—can have developmentally serious side effects on fostering creativity. Television inundates a young child's brain with second-hand images at the very time that the brain should be learning to make its own images. Storytelling feeds this developmental need beautifully; television watching suppresses it.

There are many different strategies you can use as a parent, but the bottom line on kids and screen time is this: set limits, and hold to them. The American Academy of Pediatrics recommends that parents limit children's television time to no more than two hours, and preferably one hour, per day. For some households, such limits come easily; in others they might come as a shock.

The best first step is awareness: awareness that while there's nothing wrong with television in its place, the electronic screen can cause untold developmental damage when it consumes too many of a child's waking hours.

As for the content issue, debates have been going on for years regarding how the shows kids watch affect their behavior. There have been studies and counter-studies and endless discussions about violence in particular.

But you don't need a study to realize that the entire television industry is built upon the recognition that what is shown on television does influence people's behavior. Television is a commercial medium, existing almost entirely because advertisers believe in its power to deliver their messages to large numbers of people. This is how market forces in this country have worked to create our television industry. Arguing whether this was for the benefit of our population or not is beside the point. It's the system we have, and it has its strengths and weaknesses. The point to understand is that television exists, more or less, to show us things that are supposed to affect what we do.

As parents we must be especially vigilant about content because small children soak up lessons about how the world works. Whether these lessons come from digging for salamanders in the backyard or from the pen of a Hollywood situation comedy writer depends upon us.

Computers and Creativity

What about computers? Isn't computer time different from television time? Isn't it better—less passive, more interactive, commercial-free, and more oriented toward problem solving and creativity?

In some ways, this is true. A child at a computer screen is not a completely passive viewer and is also not subject to commercial messages that may or may not be appropriate for him or her. But sitting at a computer is still sitting, and the child is still being flooded with second-hand images. Most development experts would include computer time within the one- to two-hour per day limit for screen time.

> Storytelling feeds creative development beautifully; television watching suppresses it.

There's no doubt that a home computer can provide your child with a fun and rewarding experience. Software options have multiplied in recent years, and today's basic hardware allows a level of graphic quality and responsiveness that was unheard of for consumers ten years ago. In fact, software offerings are so varied that parents are easily faced with the dilemma of too much choice and not enough reliable information for narrowing down that choice.

Software content is difficult to judge in advance. You can't scan through software like a book to get a sense of what it offers. Even if you have the chance to see it in action in the store before you buy, you can't always know how the program will play out for your children over time. In the end, most buying decisions about children's software are based on one or more of four sources of information: reviews in computer magazines, the description on the software package, your child's experience with the program in school or at a friend's house, or a friend's experience with his or her children.

You may want to consider all of these sources, but do not rely on a single source alone in making decisions about a program's quality and how much it encourages creativity. Reviews in computer magazines, even magazines purportedly geared toward families, are not uniformly trustworthy. Sometimes the reviewers fail to look at the products they write about through the eyes of a typical user. Other times reviews attempt to incorporate comments about the software from actual young users. But a six-year-old saying "I like this!" is no criterion upon which to base parental judgment. Kids love candy, too, but you don't let them eat it for breakfast, lunch, and dinner.

The packaging can give you some clues as to what's inside— but only if you learn to read between the lines. As for what you hear either from your own children or from friends, this input can be helpful if you probe beyond surface reactions. Why does your child or your friend's child like a particular program? What's enjoyable about it? How does he feel while playing with it? Is he enjoying the program's environment or merely rushing to achieve a particular goal, after which the product will lose its meaning?

One of the most serious creativity-related problems with children's software is the implicit message delivered by many that real world activities and a child's own imagination are not enough when it comes to having fun. Parents must be wary of this unspoken message and reject any software that implies a virtual world is superior to the real world.

For a creative child, there is no substitute for tactile, three-dimensional, palpable forms and for authentic smells and sensations. Creativity is a force of life and cannot develop without an intimate connection to the world around us. A creative child knows how to turn off the machines around her and feel the wonder and the joy of life itself.

CHAPTER TEN

The Role of School

"The human mind, once shaped by a new idea, never regains its original dimensions."
—OLIVER WENDELL HOLMES

We all want our children to be educated, but the process of education is complicated. Consensus on how children should be educated is hard to achieve. Educational resources can be difficult to procure. And then there's the question of evaluation: how can a parent judge what's really happening in the classroom?

Most discussions regarding quality of education have actually focused on quantity issues: how many computers a school can manage to buy, how much homework a teacher assigns, how many hours long is the school day, how quickly children learn to read. These quantitative measurements are easier to make than qualitative ones; they give parents and administrators alike a yardstick by which to compare and contrast. And no doubt some of these measurements are worthwhile.

But genuine education has far less to do with quantity than quality. This is especially true regarding the school's role in nurturing creativity—a role that is finally being recognized as important, even critical.

This is a new recognition for mainstream American education. While there are private educational systems—Montessori and Waldorf in particular—with creativity-oriented curricula, it may be the work of Harvard University educator Howard Gardner that has most notably begun expanding the views of more traditional school systems. Gardner, a creativity expert, is well known for his theory of multiple intelligences, which divides intelligence into seven distinct areas. In his book *Frames of Mind*, Gardner outlines these seven distinct types of intelligences:

- ✵ *Spatial Reasoning:* The ability to understand how things relate in space, often indicated by a skill at building things, as well as being able to imagine what something looks like from different sides.

- ✵ *Music:* An innate attraction to the world of sound. Children with musical intelligence should be given the chance to explore sounds and create their own songs.

- ✵ *Language:* A love of language; the primary intelligence behind writers, poets, lyricists, and great speakers.

- ✵ *Math and Logic:* The intelligence dominated by reasoning power. It drives the lives of those who are mathematicians and scientists.

- ✵ *Interpersonal Intelligence:* An ability to understand other people—an intelligence, says Gardner, that is routinely ignored by traditional intelligence tests.

- ✵ *Intrapersonal Intelligence:* Self-knowledge; one intelligence that tends to deepen throughout life.

- ✵ *Movement:* The capacity to use your whole body or parts of your body to solve problems or make things.

This is often the primary intelligence behind athletes, dancers, and many artists and craftspeople.

Everyone, he believes, possesses these intelligences at different levels in different combinations. Gardner resists the traditional academic view that some of these areas involve more "smarts" than others. "Why is mathematical ability called 'intelligence' and musical ability called 'talent'?" he asks.

Although Gardner's provocative ideas have not transformed many of our schools yet, they have caused many teachers and school officials around the country to contemplate changes to an educational model that has focused on the sort of intelligence that can be measured by standardized testing. This is good news for anyone hoping that our schools may play an increasingly effective role in nurturing creativity in children.

> How can parents judge what's really happening in their child's classroom?

And this idea that there are different types of intelligences has in fact been put to practical use, most notably in an Indianapolis inner-city elementary school called the Key School. There, Gardner's theories have been getting a real-life test for the past ten years. Judging by the school's overwhelming popularity and the joyfulness and motivation of its students, it has been a resoundingly successful experiment.

The Key School was designed as a racially balanced magnet school and based its educational philosophy directly upon Gardner's theory of seven intelligences. A program was designed in which students would spend a part of every day developing each of the seven areas. The idea is to let children discover the areas in which they have natural curiosity and talent and to allow them to explore these freely and with delight.

Activities at the Key School draw on several intelligences at once—much like activities in life itself. Underlying everything done at the school is the effort to stimulate the imagination and interest of the child, setting the stage for a lifetime of creativity and growth.

Gardner's theories can help point a school, such as the Key School, in the right direction when it comes to fostering creativity, but they are not a required part of the mix. While aca-

LOOSEN UP!

In many traditional educational environments, one of the biggest barriers to creativity is rigidity. Rigidity tells children there is one and only one way to do a task; rigid teachers are not open to unexpected expression, interpretation, or analysis. Rigidity also fosters monotony—a most creativity-stifling state of mind.

The environment fostered by the traditional American educational model has not only kept student creativity under wraps, but it also may have contributed to some of the problems in motivation and performance that haunt our schools. What's more, teachers and administrators bogged down in a rigid, quantitative mindset seem too often incapable of conceiving of appropriate changes. They lack the ability to design institutions that are warm, spirited, and nourishing. This ability is not a luxury; it may be a necessity.

"The American educational system is in danger not because the school day is too short or because there is not enough mathematics in the curriculum," writes learning specialist Thomas Armstrong, "but because our classrooms have become emotional wastelands. The schools must become centers of passion and purpose for children before the crisis in education is truly addressed." Schools, he insists, should be "life-affirming," rather than blindly reflective of administrative policies and entrenched academic procedures.

demic theorizing can be helpful, the ability to transform a school will always be based on two requirements: having teachers who really care about children, and having parents who really care about education. The combination of those two groups of people can go a long way toward effecting educational change. And here's the best news of all: neither of these groups is in short supply.

Evaluating Your School

In many ways, your children's education begins with you, the parent. Many child development experts are dismayed at the lack of connection they often see between parents and their children's schooling. Even parents who themselves are well educated often appear too willing to hand complete responsibility over to their children's school. They either don't realize the importance of remaining involved, don't think they have the time, don't know exactly how to start, or maybe a bit of all three.

For parents interested in assessing the level of creativity utilized by their child's school, the first step, if permitted by the school, is to visit the classroom during a normal school day. As you observe, here are a few things to ask yourself:

☼ How actively does the teacher engage with the children? Does she listen, is there give-and-take, does she ask open-ended questions? Does she encourage new perspectives? Does she teach them to question the original premise? Too much standing and lecturing at the class may be a sign of a teacher not inclined to nurture creativity.

☼ Is the class amply adorned with products of the children's creativity? A good display indicates that what the children produce is directly relevant to the curriculum and that this work is considered valuable.

✺ Is there some opportunity for the children to work in groups? Are the children ever able to interact informally during class time? Obviously classrooms need structure and decorum, but creativity flows more freely in less formal activities and when kids can more naturally move their bodies and use fuller voices. The children should not, however, appear out of control.

✺ How flexible is the teacher with unexpected ideas or circumstances? Creativity thrives in an environment that is neither rigid nor judgmental.

✺ Do the children appear animated and involved? Do they seem internally motivated, or are they pushed by external rewards for participation? While there is nothing wrong with some classroom incentives, creativity is not nurtured through a reward system. It's crucial that the motivation to create come from within the child. Teachers sensitive to this issue will be skilled at drawing out a child's inborn impulse to learn.

✺ Is everybody happy? This is not as facetious a question as it seems. A room full of kids who are consistently being inspired to be their best creative selves is a room full of spirit. Eyes will be bright, and bodies will be joyful, not squirmy or slouchy. In the right kind of classroom, you can feel the energy of a supportive community upon entering the room. It's that clear.

After the classroom visit or visits, you can apply similar questions to the school at large. Are student projects on display around the building? Do children seem lively but well behaved? Do teachers seem encouraging?

Arrange a talk with the principal, and find out about his or her educational philosophy. Ask directly about creativity: How important is creativity in the school? How does the school nurture creativity in children? Compare the principal's responses to your own observations.

Remember that no school is perfect. But perfection is not necessary for a school to offer a warm, nurturing place for children to develop their creative spirits.

Supporting Creativity

The most effective way you can work toward helping foster a creativity-friendly environment in your school is to be involved. It's that simple—and that complicated. Many parents are pressed for time. Despite many good intentions, it's all many parents can do to be sure that their children are delivered to and from school at the appropriate times. Making time for classroom visits or information-getting phone calls with teachers can be a logistical problem.

But being involved doesn't necessarily mean you must become a classroom parent or haunt the hallways of the school seeking projects to coordinate. Being in regular contact with the teacher, either through written notes or telephone calls, is a way of being involved. Sitting down with your child to look at her homework each day is a way of being involved. Engaging your child in a meaningful discussion about her school day beyond "What did you do at school today?"—to which the inevitable reply is "Nothing"—is also a way of being involved. Better questions are open-ended, such as, "What was the most interesting (or frustrating, exciting, funny, etc.) thing that happened in school today?"

It's important to approach any involvement in the school with a positive attitude. Most teachers and administrators are doing their best with the available resources and mean to serve the interests of the children. Most schools, in fact, are open to hearing from parents who arrive with constructive comments.

Not every school is likely to be a paragon of creativity orientation. But most schools have many positive attributes that can be bolstered. In the end, how well your child's creativity is fostered at school is related to how well it has been fostered at home—and how well it is fostered by society at large. We in this country sometimes expect too much from our schools, as Howard Gardner points out:

> It's mythological to think that we can change the schools and leave the rest of society the way that it is. If you think about it, the schools are intimately connected with the other aspects of society—the other kinds of institutions, other kinds of civic challenges, other kinds of world challenges—and I don't think we can have a school system that's qualitatively different unless we have a society that's qualitatively different.

CHAPTER ELEVEN

Creative for Life

"It is the learners who inherit the future. The learned usually find themselves equipped to live in a world that no longer exists."

—ERIC HOFFER

A four-year-old inventing funny sounds. A seven-year-old creating a town on the driveway. A two-year-old reveling in the connection between rhythm and movement. Creativity in childhood, as we've now seen firsthand, can take many wondrous forms. And it can lead to many wonderful, memorable childhood moments.

But when all is said and done, what do these moments add up to? How can we be sure that a child whose creative spirit has been nurtured throughout his childhood will have a richer, more rewarding life as an adult?

Well, there are certainly no statistics to prove this. But we have the informed observations of a consensus of thinkers and experts both from today and from years gone by. Few people who have pondered the concept of creativity doubt the connection between a fulfilling childhood of imaginative play and a fruitful adulthood.

"A great man," wrote the ancient Chinese philosopher Meng-tzu, "is he who has not lost the heart of a child."

This is what today's creativity consultants are being paid to help American adults understand. Your child is in the enviable position of being in this frame of mind now, knowing instinctively that creativity and fun go hand in hand. You, in turn, have the wonderful job of recognizing this joyful, creative heart in its pure form, of nurturing it through its developing years.

"No one could have foreseen that children had concealed within themselves a vital secret capable of lifting the veil that covered the human soul," wrote educator Maria Montessori,

> To teach creativity, you must reinvigorate the child's heart within yourself.

"that they carried within themselves something which, if discovered, would help adults to solve their own individual and social problems."

Therein lies the key to our final discussion. All the topics we've covered, all the activities we've described, are a great start. But underneath it all, underneath your parental responsibility to promote and encourage and nurture creativity in your child, is an unexpected but critical message: you must nurture your own creativity as well. In addition to keeping your child in touch with his innate creative spirit, you must reinvigorate the child's heart within yourself.

How better, after all, to generate in the home the pervasive atmosphere that creativity is important, is delighted in—that creativity matters, that it enriches our lives. In such a home, ideas are not judged and passions are encouraged. Silliness is not only tolerated, it's advisable. New perspectives are always in demand, conventional premises always subject to questioning.

Children are, in some ways, the perfect "excuse" for adults to reconnect to their creative selves. You might feel it too odd to take a walk splashing through puddles on a rainy day by yourself, but if you've got a child along, no one will raise an eyebrow. You might feel downright foolish kicking up a storm of falling leaves, pretending to be the wind, but grab a child or two, head out to the park, and voilà!— instant freedom and joy. Creativity is the language of joy. Joy is a powerful life force.

Creativity is a gift. We all receive it at birth, but we must practice it in order to keep it. To feel the power of its presence not only as a child but also as an adult is to feel truly alive, capable of being the very best one can be. It is to be alive in a world ever vibrant with possibility, with hope, with wonder.

"Whatever you can do or dream you can, begin it," wrote the extraordinary German poet and philosopher Goethe. "Boldness has genius, power, and magic in it. Begin it now."

Index

Specific activities and games by name are in boldface type. Categories of activities and games are in italic.

Acting and performing: activities, 121–122, 125, 127; physical aspect of, 39

Acting out versus creativity, 12, 18, 50–54

Activities and games; about, 54, 57–58; age appropriateness, 57–58; creative behavior checklist, 58; "formal" games, 35, 109; "hands-on" aspects, 39; rules and, 37, 51

Adulthood: creativity in, 6–7, 183–185; link between creative childhood and, 12–13

Adults and parents: clever combinations, 47; correcting the child, 36; creativity, attitudes of, 12, 45–48; creativity versus acting out, 12, 18, 50–54; labeling and pigeonholing, 37, 55; listening versus guiding, 35–36, 48–49; media, strategies for using, 167–173; patience, 49; perseverance and creativity, inspiring, 49; playfulness, maintaining spirit of, 46; rules, 37, 47, 51; school, involvement in,

181–182; self-regulation, teaching of, 51, 53; silly substitutes, 47; structured learning, avoiding appearance of, 44, 57; surroundings, consideration of, 45–46; tolerance, 49; turning on your creativity, 47–48, 184; unconventionality, acceptance of, 49; wonder, rekindling sense of, 46

Age appropriateness for activities and games, 57–58

Age groups. *See* Preschoolers; Kindergartners; 1st and 2nd graders; 3rd graders and older

Alien Invasion, 68–69

Alphabet activities: arts, crafts, and projects, 103; imagination games, 73

Alphabet Poster, 103

American educational system, 176–179; Armstrong on, 178

Animal Day, 62

Animals: arts, crafts, and projects, 87–88; imagination games, 62; storytelling, performance, and fantasy activities, 127

Anti-Puppet Show, 121–122

Armstrong, Thomas, 178

Around the House, 151

Art tables and boxes, 37–38